DON'T CHOKE

DON'T CHOKE

A CHAMPION'S GUIDE TO WINNING UNDER PRESSURE

GARY PLAYER

with

Michael Vlismas

Skyhorse Publishing

Skyhorse Publishing books may be purchased in bulk at special discounts for sales promotion, corporate gifts, fund-raising, or educational purposes. Special editions can also be created to specifications. For details, contact Special Sales Department, Skyhorse Publishing, 555 Eighth Avenue, Suite 903, New York, NY 10018 or info@skyhorsepublishing.com.

www.skyhorsepublishing.com

10 9 8 7 6 5 4 3 2

All photos appear courtesy of Black Knight International's archives

Library of Congress Cataloging-in-Publication Data
Player, Gary.
Don't choke : a champion's guide to winning under pressure / Gary Player.
    p. cm.
Includes bibliographical references and index.
ISBN 978-1-61608-038-9
1. Golf. 2. Success. 3. Player, Gary. I. Title.
GV965.P572 2010
796.352--dc22

                                    2010005293

Printed in China

CONTENTS

The virtue of all achievement is victory over oneself. Those who know
this victory can never know defeat.

—A. J. Cronin

All good things . . . come by grace and grace comes by art and art
does not come easy.

—Norman Maclean

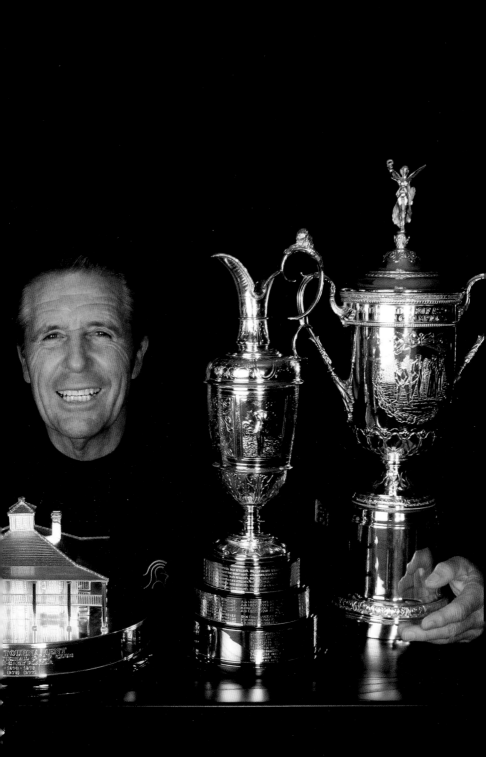

FOREWORD

If there is one thing that is perfectly clear to me after thirty-five years of working with the greatest athletes, golfers, and businessmen in the world, it is that everyone feels pressure. To learn how to handle, enjoy, and thrive on pressure, you have to be willing to choke. With time, experience, a great deal of self-reflection, and honest self-understanding, anyone can learn how to thrive on pressure.

The great competitors actually learn to perform better in pressure situations than in casual ones. But even the best will still occasionally choke and then have to relearn their lessons. It is not something you ever master or own.

There is no sense in trying to learn all of the lessons of life the hard way—from your own personal experience. It is much more efficient to learn from the experience of others who have been successful in competitive situations.

Who better to have as a teacher than one of the greatest golfers of all time, a man with a reputation for being fiery, tough, and resilient—Gary Player?

Here, Gary shares how what he learned from golf can help you with personal and business success. He is an ideal role model and teacher, as it is universally agreed that he has maintained an infectiously positive and enthusiastic attitude throughout his life. Gary has managed to combine a great marriage and family while succeeding in golf and business.

Gary had to work hard and earn everything he has achieved. Nothing came easily or readily to him. Most of what he achieved came through self-discipline, perseverance, and determination. He competed in a golden age of golf against the very best. Gary certainly won his share and was beaten many times. But he always battled on, showed tremendous resiliency, and ultimately won at life.

When I think of Gary Player the golfer, I see a man with the mind of Jack Nicklaus and Tiger Woods; the persistence, desire, and dedication of Ben Hogan and Tom Kite; the friendliness and sense of appreciation of Byron Nelson and Arnold Palmer; and the enthusiasm of the Energizer Bunny.

In this book, Gary makes it clear that he really gets it and actually lived it. He teaches that the antidote to cracking under pressure begins with a willingness to jump into the fire and let the flames burn the impurities away. Gary teaches lessons about having a healthy perspective, playing against yourself and the golf course, respecting your own game, going out and executing your game plan, and controlling the stuff you can control and not worrying about what you can't control.

Gary makes it clear that sometimes you do all the right things and someone still beats you. But the real challenge is not to beat yourself. It's knowing the difference between getting beat and beating yourself. It's knowing that everyone who competes has choked and that you must accept it when it happens. But the best learn from the experience rather than simply repeat the same errors.

Gary teaches that a resiliency to failure is actually to love getting in the hunt and finding out if you can pass the test. He makes it clear that you are a winner if you give it your best regardless of the outcome. He demonstrates that learning how to win is teachable. It is difficult. It is challenging. It takes a strong resolve, a sustained discipline, and a commitment filled with passion. But he also shows you that these are the qualities that build personal pride and confidence.

In my mind what Gary has done in the pages that follow is to tell people the honest truth—that one of the greatest challenges in life is to admit to yourself that you want something badly, dare to believe you can do it, and then go out and get yourself to do whatever it is you need to do to get whatever it is that you want. It is easy to want something and then be overcome by the fear that no matter how hard you work, you will never get what you want.

For most people, when possibilities and dreams encounter doubts and fears, it is the moment of truth. These are the defining moments that determine if you will go after it or run away and give up on your dreams, yourself, and your life.

Gary is wonderfully honest. The journey at times can be tough. It will challenge you, but it will also excite you, get you up in the morning, and give you a reason for living with enthusiasm. These are the experiences that create feelings of pride and self-satisfaction. He makes it clear that hard work and persistence are big pieces of the puzzle, but so is learning the right lessons from your experience and the experiences of others. Fortunately for us, Gary has been willing to share his lifetime learning in a most honest and frank way.

—Dr. Bob Rotella

Sports psychologist and best-selling author

December 2009

Gary Player

1

PREFACE

The greatest ambition of my life was always to be a world champion. It drove me to the far corners of the globe playing the game I loved. I enjoyed moments of great success, and I worked through others of agonizing defeat.

But what carried me through it all was a strength of mind that I was as good as I believed I could be and that nothing was impossible.

I learned very early in my career that pure talent will get you only so far, before the mind takes over and leads a person into that realm of perfection.

When the body fails or is weary, and that shot into a howling gale seems impossible, it is the mind that enables a player to pull it off.

This book is the story of my mind.

It is the story of a boy who grew up with no head start in life but had the grace of being blessed with a heart for dreams and a mind to carry him there.

As the American author David Grayson wrote of happiness, "She loves to see men at work. She loves sweat, weariness, self-sacrifice."

If anything, may the success of my eighteen Major championships and the lessons in this book teach you that nothing is impossible, as long as you go at it with everything you've got.

—**Gary Player**
Colesberg, South Africa *2009*

DON'T CHOKE

INTRODUCTION: TEEING OFF

I was coming to the end of the 7,252-yard monster that is Carnoustie in the 1968 British Open. The wind was howling. In that final round, Billy Casper, Bob Charles, and I were tied for the lead at two under par, and there were five of us within one stroke of the lead. And before me the par-five 14th hole unfolded like 483 yards of sheer green beast.

On that day, this was a golf course in a mean mood. It was not going to give up on trying to grind us into the dirt, and this was the hole that could do it to you. I stood at my drive, wrestling with the decision as to whether to go for the green with my second shot and try to carry the fearsome "Spectacles" bunkers or to play safe.

I was hitting the shot blind. Jack Nicklaus was my playing partner. He had just hit a brilliant recovery shot and was pushing hard to win the tournament. He, as well as a host of other players, would pounce on the first mistake I made, and that would be it.

I reached for a three wood and stood over the ball. Now came that moment. That moment when the entire world condenses into a dimpled, little sphere at your feet. When everything you are, and hope to become, crushes down upon you in the confined arc of a golf swing.

Do you want to know what was going through my mind? It's simple, really. I saw a nine-year-old boy sitting on a bench in the freezing cold of a winter's morning in Johannesburg, South Africa. He waits for a tram to take him across town, where he then walks to catch a bus as part of a long journey just to get to school. It's still dark, and he sits on that bench alone. His father is working deep in the gold mines. His mother had passed away from cancer. His older brother is far away fighting a world war. His sister is at boarding school. His only friend is an elderly black gentleman named John Mashaba, who makes him breakfast and dinner in the evenings, when he returns home to a dark house. And as he sits on that bench, the boy says to himself, "Someday, I'm going to be a world champion."

When I stood over that three wood, "someday" had arrived. Just as it had at four previous Major championships.

I hit possibly the finest shot of my life right there, and the ball finished fourteen inches from the hole. I holed the eagle putt for a two-shot lead, which I managed to hang on to and go on to victory.

Over the years, I've heard people say, "That Gary Player was certainly lucky in his career." But if it was just luck, how come I kept doing it? And how come Nicklaus kept doing it? And Ben Hogan, Sam Snead, and now Tiger Woods? It's not luck. It's the ability to bring something out of yourself when it's really necessary and when it counts. That's the difference between being very good, a star, and a superstar.

People use the word "superstar" very loosely these days. But there is a vast difference between the very good player and the superstar.

Sure, there have been many very good players who have actually played better than the superstars. A good example of this was Tom Weiskopf. In my opinion, Tom was a better striker of a golf ball than Jack Nicklaus was. He was a better golfer than Arnold Palmer, too, and most of the other golfers of my time. Yet Weiskopf won only one Major championship on the regular tour and one on the senior tour.

If you had given me Weiskopf's natural ability to play the game, I might have won twenty-five Majors. But what Weiskopf lacked was the necessary ingredients to take him into that superstar category. The same ingredients that players like Nicklaus had.

I've seen this time and time again in my fifty-six years as a professional golfer. People always talk about a player's beautiful swing or how far he hits the ball. But a beautiful swing doesn't win Major championships, a great putter does.

There are a few ingredients—and I don't know whether they're God-given gifts or passed on genetically—but you need a great passion, an enjoyment of suffering, the ability to accept adversity in the right light, to not to feel sorry for yourself, to not to be negative, and a good nerve.

It's all pieces of a puzzle that make a Major champion.

Yes, there is an element of luck. But luck is the residue of design. And in my life, when you got right down to the bare bones of it, sheer determination often carried me through.

Guts can manifest itself in myriad ways.

So here are my eighteen Major championships and the lessons I learned from each one that helped make them special and that will, I hope, help you in life and business when you stand with that three wood in your hand, stare down the beast, and seek victory.

Gary Player

WHAT DEFINES CHOKING?

1

Everybody has nerves. So, in a sense, all of us are potential chokers. Some just choke less than others. Or to put it another way, some have more control of their nerves than others. But what is it that separates those who rise to the challenge and those who crack under the pressure?

In my fifty-six years of playing professional golf, I have had more than enough time to make a careful study of what the qualities of a great champion are. I've seen players with the most amazing natural ability who never came close to realizing their potential, and I've seen players take lousy swings and win time and time again. It was often said of my own career that I had done more with less than any golfer before me.

I certainly didn't have a great swing when I started out. But give me a lousy swing and the ability to win under pressure any day over a swing that looks good but doesn't get the job done. After all, the ultimate divider in this game is not how beautiful

your swing is. It's what you win. My bank manager never asked me how I was swinging; he asked what I was depositing.

So the conclusion that I've come to is that a player has no greater asset on the golf course than the power of his mind. The decisions are made in the mind first; only then do the body, club, and ball follow.

Most players have natural ability. I don't think Tiger Woods has much more ability than the other top five players in the world. But on the course he has much more control of his nerves. Why? Why did I, or Jack Nicklaus, when we were coming down the stretch with a chance to win a Major championship not choke?

For a start, when I came down the line in a Major championship, I was mentally prepared. I knew I was tied with Tom Watson or Lee Trevino or Nicklaus, and I wasn't going to let myself choke. Perspective was also key for me. I would remind myself, "What right do you have to be nervous? There are people suffering all over the world, people who are dying of starvation, and you're one of the lucky ones to be in this position to win a Major." I also used meditation to help overcome pressure, and it was a big part of my success. As I have said many times, "Plant a seed and it grows."

The mind is what makes you a superstar, and what your mind feeds you with determines the outcome. But there is a fine line between what people call choking and just plain bad course management, poor decisions, or the effect of some other basic flaw.

There have been golfers who had big leads in Major championships and were swinging extremely well for the first three days, then blew it in the final round. That, in my opinion, is a result of nerves. They hadn't trained themselves sufficiently to know how to handle their nerves in that situation.

Greg Norman, when he had a six-shot lead over Nick Faldo in the 1996 Masters, played so poorly on the last day compared with the beautiful golf he displayed the previous three days because, in my opinion, his mind fed him the wrong thoughts.

In the early part of Tom Watson's career, there were times when he had a chance to win, and he couldn't carry it through. People labeled him a choker. I can state categorically that Tom Watson was never a choker.

Watson has a superb mind for golf. If you put Watson's head on Norman's body, Norman would've won six Majors. But when Tom went through that stretch where he didn't win for ten years, he was battling with the yips. The great golf writer Henry Longhurst said, "If you get the yips, you die with the yips." Watson was so strong mentally that he overcame the yips.

In my opinion, there were also flaws in his swing, and once he corrected these, he went on to become a superstar. At some point in all of our careers we had flaws.

Then you look at a man like Seve Ballesteros. He was not an accurate driver of the ball. But he won. He often brought his "C" game to Majors and still won them. It was because his mind didn't allow him to believe he was actually hitting the ball that badly.

There are countless examples of the difference between choking and poor decision making. The 2006 US Open at Winged Foot is a good one. Colin Montgomerie needed only a bogey on the final hole to tie for the lead, and he couldn't make it. That's nerves. But then Phil Mickelson, who hit only two fairways the whole day, decided to take a driver off the final tee, to disastrous consequences that ultimately cost him a shot at the title. He should have gone with an iron off the tee. That's just bad course management.

When in a similar position with a chance to win a Major. I never saw Nicklaus make that kind of error.

I did see Arnold Palmer hold a six-shot lead with nine holes to go in the 1966 US Open at Olympic in San Francisco, and Billy Casper beat him. Arnold was a very aggressive player. But he kept shooting at the flags with a six-shot lead. He was fed the wrong information by his mind. He should have been going for the middle of the greens and making his pars. That way, he couldn't lose. But he kept charging, which was his nature. He accepted it as such because that was how he played the game. This was completely opposite to Jack Nicklaus's strategy. Arnold played to his temperament; if he had played it safe, he might not have won seven Majors.

There's a difference between what Palmer did, what Norman did, and what Mickelson did when they had chances to win Majors and didn't close out, though. Although it may appear so, choking is not something that just suddenly happens. It's a gradual process of negative thinking that eventually manifests itself under pressure. And for this reason it can be overcome by training your mind in a positive process. If you prepare, do your homework, and go through the necessary experiences with the right mind-set, choking should not enter the equation.

The way I programmed my mind to avoid choking was like self-hypnosis. I did not allow choking to even factor into my thinking. I trained myself to enjoy every challenge.

Yes, there are a number of ingredients that go into the making of a champion. You've got to have the passion. You've got to actually enjoy suffering, and you've got to be prepared to make the necessary sacrifices it takes to succeed.

And most important, you can't feel sorry for yourself.

But eventually it all comes down to how well you handle the pressure. And at the Major championship level, the pressure is almost unbearable. As Bobby Locke described it, "The competition is utterly ruthless."

I must point out that there is no disgrace in your nerve not being that strong to start with. After all, we're only human. And don't ever think there weren't times when I wasn't nervous. I'll never forget the 1962 Masters and the play-off I was facing with Arnold Palmer and Dow Finsterwald. Before that round, I actually had something of a mental block about just going to the golf course. As I stood on the first tee, I just saw hoards of people lining the fairway on both sides from tee to green. Yes, I was nervous. But I never let it stop me from opening with a birdie on that first hole.

Match play is a perfect format for exposing a golfer's nerves. My match with Tony Lema in the 1965 World Match Play Championship represented everything of the character and mental approach I brought to my game. In a sense, this match summed up my whole life.

After nineteen holes I was a massive seven holes down to Lema. But I fought my way back to win on the 37th hole. When I started that fight back, I saw the change in Lema. He went from talking quite a bit during the match and feeling very relaxed to getting quiet and more worried as it wore on. But I was still five down with nine holes to play.

I birdied 10, 11, and 13 to pull within two shots of Lema. By that point, Lema had stopped talking. And somewhere, deep in the mind of this good player, that thought started to creep in: "I might lose." That's all it takes in a pressure situation. That one negative thought. I won that match. It took everything out of me mentally and physically, but I was prepared to go and fetch everything deep inside me to throw at Lema and what seemed like an impossible position to come back from.

That has been the story of my life in golf. Don't give up. Don't surrender. Don't quit. Don't choke.

I proved that you are able to train your mind to strengthen your nerve.

And I can tell you that golf is in its infancy concerning the power of the mind. All you ever hear and read is what a beautiful swing so and so has and what a long ball he hits. You drive for show and putt for dough. Give me the man with a good mind and a great putter any day.

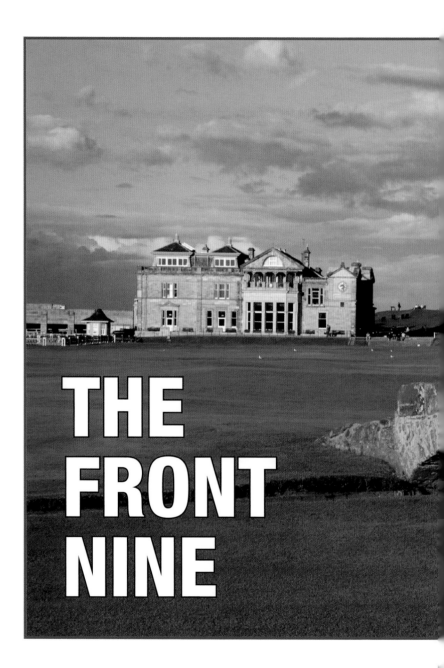

THE FRONT NINE

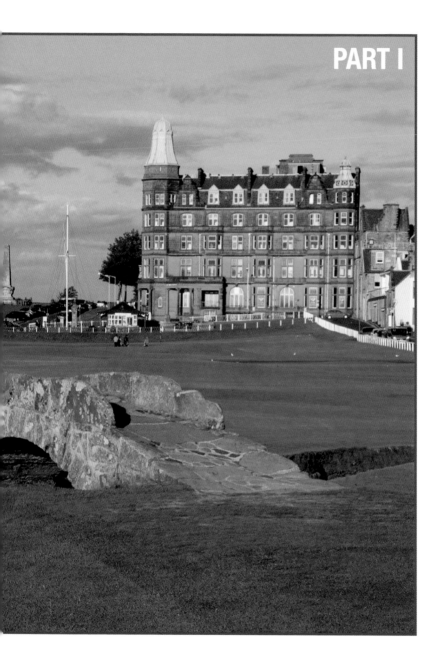

PART I

NEVER, NEVER, NEVER GIVE UP

Gary Player 1

Well, how's that for being a shorty?

—Dr. Ian Player

1959 BRITISH OPEN:
MUIRFIELD, SCOTLAND

The first one is always hard, and so it was for me, purely because I had worked myself to the bone to get to this point of winning my first Major.

There are degrees of success, and I arrived at Muirfield in Scotland having fulfilled most of these as a tournament winner around the world. But that was never going to be enough for me. I had to win Majors, to say I had beaten the best in the world at the game's highest level.

It's safe to say I made a disastrous start to this one, opening with a 75 that left me seven shots off the first round lead.

I battled my way through the next rounds, but I was still in no great shape going into the final day.

That evening I attended a dinner that the president of Slazenger, Humphrey McMaster, also attended. I remember walking up to his table and saying, "Mr. McMaster, tomorrow I am going to win the Open." He looked at me in disbelief and replied, "Young man, at your age? And besides, you're six shots back."

Willie Auchterlonie was twenty-one when he won the 1893 Open. Young Tom Morris was seventeen when he won the Open in 1868. And here I was, twenty-three years old, six shots back, and saying I was going to win. Why not?

Then the moment came. I was playing the final hole, and all I needed was a par four to win the tournament. It would've given me the 66 I had set for myself as a target at the start of the round. The 66 I knew would win me the Open and change my life forever.

I made six.

My whole world collapsed on me right there. There is a famous photograph of me with my head in my hands and my wife, Vivienne, trying to console me. It took all of my resolve just to sign my scorecard.

Because I was so far behind at the start of the round, I finished much earlier than the rest of the field. So I left the golf course and headed straight for my hotel, convinced that I had thrown away the Open Championship.

I didn't choke on that last hole. The weather was terrible, and the wind was howling. That 18th fairway was very narrow, and I hit a drive that just crept into the bunker. I hit it out and hit the third on the front edge of the green, because the wind was blowing so hard, and then I three-putted.

But I had shot 284 in those conditions, and it proved too much for the rest of the field to match. I received a phone call from the course to inform me that I had won the Open and could come and collect the Claret Jug at the official prize giving.

At last, I was the Open champion. I had broken through with my first Major.

THE CHOKE CHALLENGE

Breaking through for the first time brings with it a whole different set of pressures. I understood the pressure of Major championship golf. A year before Muirfield, I had finished second in the US Open, and I'd had top-ten finishes in the Open in 1958 and the Masters in 1959. But this was new in terms of dealing with the pressure of trying to become a Major championship winner for the first time in my career.

It's a case of dealing with the nerves of realizing a dream for the first time. That can be a major obstacle when you want something so badly and have worked all your life to be at that point. The secret is to focus not on the pressure of the situation but rather on the blessing of being in a position to go for your dream. And often, at the moment when it looks as if that dream has fallen to pieces right in front of your eyes, that's when the phone call comes.

MAJOR MENTALITY

Never think you are too young to succeed. One of my favorite stories is that of David and Goliath. While there is much speculation on the age of David when he slew Goliath in battle, most experts agree that he was probably a teenager. So a teenager achieved what an entire army of experienced soldiers was too afraid to do. This is the beauty of youth, in that you have not yet had the time to become afraid or cautious of bigger situations. Use your youth to your advantage. There is a natural confidence in youth that should never be under-estimated. Dream your dreams and then have the courage to go out there and make them happen.

SLAYING
THE GIANTS

Gary Player

1

The test of courage comes when we are in the minority.
—Ralph Sockman

1961 MASTERS:
AUGUSTA NATIONAL GOLF CLUB, GEORGIA

Arnold Palmer was building his reputation, and he was at the height of his powers in the sixties. By 1961 he had already won three Majors (two Masters titles and one US Open) and a host of other tournaments.

In 1960, he had a memorable season in which he won eight tournaments, including the Masters and the US Open. And he won those two Majors in his usual spectacular style, playing the bold, aggressive golf that was his trademark. By the time of the 1961 Masters, Arnold was on his way to becoming the first player to earn $100,000 in a single season.

To his fans, he was "The King." To golf, he was the man who popularized the game like none before him. People flocked to watch him play, and they became known as "Arnie's Army." They loved his aggressive nature in tournaments. So much so that they coined the phrase "The Palmer Charge" to describe his last-minute runs at victory.

And into all of this, along comes a young upstart from a country most Americans had never heard of, and he's challenging their hero. I can tell you, if there were one hundred thousand fans at the tournament that week, there were only two pulling for me—my wife and my dog.

I had made a name for myself, though, and coming into the Masters I was at the top of the PGA Tour's money list despite Arnold having won three of his first eight tournaments that year. But this wasn't just another tournament. This was the Masters, and Arnold Palmer was back to defend his title in front of his adoring fans.

The Americans were screaming for Arnold to win that week. In situations like that, it's very easy to feel intimidated. You can start feeling sorry for yourself and ask, "Why are they against me?" Arnold was a giant in the game, and any young golfer would've felt that presence looming over him.

But I loved it. I told myself that the more they scream for Arnold, the better I'm going to play.

I grew up tough, and that teaches you to know a challenge when you see one. And here I had a challenge. We had a great battle. I shot two rounds of 69 and 68, and Arnold posted two rounds of 68 and 69, tying us for the lead at the halfway stage.

I moved ahead with a 69 in the third round while Arnold struggled to a 73. And then it arrived—that moment when you leave the golf course, get back to your room, and close the door.

You climb into bed, and suddenly all is silent. You are away from the noise of a Major, which can be a tremendous distraction. Now it's just you and your thoughts, and in that moment before sleep all manner of things go through your mind. You just cannot stop thinking about the four-stroke lead you have over Arnold Palmer, one of the greatest players in the game, and the tremendous opportunity you have to win your second Major.

That thought can either paralyze you or motivate you. I always used it to motivate me. If there wasn't enough pressure on me, Sunday's final round was washed out, forcing it to be postponed to Monday.

I kept my focus during that final round and made a great up-and-down from the bunker on the last hole to save par. Arnold went into that same bunker and ended up making a six. In my fourth shot at it, I was the Masters champion. And not just any Masters champion. I had become the first foreign-born winner of the Masters since the birth of this Major under its current title in 1939.

It took until 1980 for there to be another foreign-born winner of the Masters besides me, and that was Seve Ballesteros.

THE CHOKE CHALLENGE

A key moment for me was that Saturday night when I went to sleep on a four-shot lead. It would have been easy to fall into the trap of obsessing about the fact that I was leading by four shots over one of the greatest golfers in the game in one of the greatest tournaments in the game. And without realizing it, the reality of the situation could've turned into a paralyzing fear. So I had to teach myself to relax.

I went to bed that night knowing I was leading by four shots, but I turned it into a positive by telling myself, "Tomorrow, I have the chance to become the first foreign winner of the Masters. Man, I'm going to win it." It was all filled with a positive vibe. I couldn't wait for the challenge. I made sure I didn't have the time to worry about nerves and choking.

In the end, I had beaten Arnold Palmer. But more important, I had beaten the aura around him as well. This ability to crush the negative by turning it into something positive shone through in another tournament before this as well.

In 1956 I was invited to play in the Ampol Tournament in Melbourne, Australia, which was being held at the same time as

This is a "Marriage—and £5,000" Jump for Joy: and it's the Year's HAPPIEST Picture

[handwritten: "How are you?" "to Malcolm"]

"Sunday Times" Reporter
VEREENIGING, Saturday. — "The happiest girl in South Africa" was how 19-year-old, brunette Vivienne Verwey, described herself at the Maccauvlei golf course, across the Vaal River from Vereeniging, to-day.

The reason: Young (21) Gary Player, her fiancé and South Africa's "successor to Bobby Locke", had won the £5,000 first prize in the Ampol golf tournament at Yarra Yarra, Australia. And before he won he declared: "If I win, I will marry Vivienne immediately."

Vivienne told me: "This is the sort of thing one dreams about but never quite believes will happen. Gary has been playing superb golf lately. Call it a woman's intuition if you like, but I had a strange feeling that he would win."

Go Overseas With Him

Final plans for the wedding would be made when Gary Player arrived home early in December, she said.

(Meanwhile a cable from Gary was on its way to her reading: "We've won £5,000 and will marry immediately.")

"But nothing can be decided then — I can only say that the wedding will be before the South African Open in April.

"After that Gary will make for England, where he will compete in the British Open. When the time comes, he will make a bid for the Tam 'O Shanter tournament in America."

Vivienne is determined to accompany Gary Player on his next overseas trip. She will not be left behind so soon after the marriage, she said.

An outstanding golfer in own right, she will be able to hold her own in any company if she does go overseas.

Mrs. Verwey, Vivienne's mother, was also at Maccauvlei, where 15-year-old Bobby, her son and the newest South African golfing prodigy, was competing in a tournament. "I know they will be very happy," she said.

Earlier, Bobby had been defeated two and one by the burly, long-hitting Peter Vorster (Bloemfontein) in the Maccauvlei tournament.

Nineteen-year-old Vivienne Verwey jumps with joy at the Maccauvlei golf course, Vereeniging, yesterday, when she hears that her fiance, Gary Player, had won the £5,000 Ampol golf tournament in Melbourne, Australia. Before the match Gary declared: "If I win, I will marry Vivienne

This picture, taken as Vivienne received news of Gary's victory that ensured they were financially able to marry, received an award for news photograph of the year.

the Olympic Games. It offered the largest prize money—£5,000 first prize—in the world outside of America. Five thousand pounds was a fortune in those days.

I told Vivienne, then my fiancée, "If I win this tournament, I'll come back to South Africa, and we'll get married."

I was leading the tournament by four shots with one round to play. You can imagine how badly I wanted to win the tournament. Then it rained, and the final round was postponed to Monday. I spent a lot of that Sunday visualizing and preparing how I would go about winning.

That Sunday evening I was in my hotel room. There was a connecting door to another room. I was practicing my putting against this door and hitting putt after putt against it. The next thing I know the door opens, and Jack Kramer—one of the greatest tennis players in the game—is standing there. The first

thing he said was, "What the hell is going on here?" Then he saw me and said, "Gary, what's wrong with you?" I said to him, "Jack, I'm leading the tournament by four shots, and I'm practicing because I'm going to hole a lot of putts on the final day."

And he turned around and said, "Oh, well keep going then."

I won the tournament. Instead of sitting there worrying about my four-shot lead, I was doing something positive and practicing.

And by the way, after my victory I sent Vivienne a telegram that said, "Buy the dress. We're getting married."

MAJOR MENTALITY

It's easy to become paralyzed by a fear of the challenge before you, and what most people tend to do when faced with such a challenge is ask, "Why me?"

The fact that you are there, in that cauldron of competition, in front of this challenge, should be your answer. You are there because you want to be there, because it's your dream to be there, and you need to see that challenge in the same light. To be great, you have to do great things. And great things wouldn't be the ultimate prizes they are if they didn't come with great challenges.

A saying I've always loved is "Be careful what you wish for, you just might get it." Don't be afraid of realizing your goals and dreams. If you are, they will remain simple wishes that you daydream about, and they'll never become the reality of a goal achieved.

Gary Player

TOUGH TIMES AREN'T ALWAYS BAD TIMES

Out of the night that covers me,
Black as the pit from pole to pole,
I thank whatever gods may be
For my unconquerable soul.

—William Ernest Henley

1962 PGA CHAMPIONSHIP:
ARONIMINK GOLF CLUB, PENNSYLVANIA

Two choices. That's pretty much what it comes down to for me.

In every situation in life you have two choices: You can be positive, or you can be negative.

As I sat on a plane soaring over the Atlantic, I had to choose. I had just missed the cut in the Open Championship at Royal Troon. It's true that Troon that year was a terrifying prospect. The course was bone dry, and the bad bounces so typical of links golf all found their way to me that week.

And I'll tell you something: On one of the few occasions in my life, while battling through a miserable Open experience, I just reached a point where I couldn't go on. That course had me beat, and everything I tried felt pointless.

And bang went the Open as a result.

It was a hard blow in what had been a hard year for me. I finished second in the Masters, and while this may sound like nothing to get too worked up about, I really felt I deserved to win that one more than I did the previous year. Then I finished sixth in the US Open. But I wasn't winning.

Then came the blow of Troon.

I needed to make a four on the last hole of the second round to make the cut. On the 18th there is out of bounds just at the back of the green, and another one of those bad bounces I'd had all week took its toll again here. My ball finished an inch out of bounds, and I missed the cut by one stroke.

So there I sat, on a plane flying over to my next Major—the PGA Championship at Aronimink—with a reasonably positive mind. I had left the Open Championship with my tail between my legs. That's how I described it to a few journalists at the time, and that's how I was quoted in the newspapers. Now the whole golf world knew it. I had two choices, and on that plane I was already a long way down the road toward the one choice that doesn't win you a club championship, never mind a Major. So I made the switch.

I got back the passion and the hunger that have always driven me. I decided that I couldn't wait to get to the next tournament

to redeem myself. I analyzed what I did wrong at Troon and put it behind me.

I had never before set foot on the course at Aronimink, but before I arrived I said to myself, "I'm going to love that golf course. I'm going to love that place." I prepared myself mentally. I made up my mind that it was going to be a great week for me, and I visualized myself winning the PGA Championship. I didn't wait. I got on the earliest flight possible to Philadelphia to make sure I outpracticed everyone. I never wanted anybody to hit more balls than me. I learned this from Ben Hogan and have watched strong players like Tom Kite and Vijay Singh take that same lesson to heart.

I went to the golf course early and practiced hard, working out my strategy for the week and building up my confidence.

On the final hole of the tournament, I hit an amazing shot from the worst possible position. My drive was right and in the trees, but I took a three wood and sliced it around the corner and onto the green about thirty feet from the pin.

My first putt finished not far from the hole. In the end, it was a short putt that sealed a one-shot victory for me over Bob Goalby, my first in fifteen months. But the truth is that there was actually a chasm of soul searching within those few inches between the ball and hole on that final putt, and I was glad to have crossed it in the way I did. Bob Goalby was a fine competitor, and we had an exciting battle.

THE CHOKE CHALLENGE

Two choices. I had made the shift in my mind on that plane trip over to Aronimink. And I rubber-stamped it with my game.

That three wood on the last hole was a pure case of me just crushing any negative thought in my head. You have two choices in everything, yet it's amazing how many people choose to be negative and miserable.

Adversity was one of the great motivators for me in winning all my Major championships.

I've been to visit children in squatter camps with no running water and no beds to sleep in, but they all tell me they want to be doctors, lawyers, and even president of the country. These children have nothing, but they want to be everything. Yet other people have everything and choose to be nothing.

All of us face adversities on a daily basis. In his book *A Good Walk Spoiled*, John Feinstein explains the fear every professional lives with of suddenly waking up one morning and never knowing when it's going to get better.

"Any player going through tough times worries that he is about to become one of those guys whose name is whispered around the locker room in the way people talk about the recently dead," Feinstein wrote.

This is the player who stands over three-foot putts thinking about how his contracting business is going to survive the winter or whether he should take that job as an insurance salesman to supplement his income, what with the new baby coming and all. Some come out of it because of their sheer mental strength. Some never do. Those who make it know that adversity is a fact of life. It will always be there, and you need to find a way to live with it and roll with the punches, rather than fight against it. And realize that everybody has bad times.

MAJOR MENTALITY

The beauty of golf is the "one shot at a time" philosophy it engenders. It forces you to focus on the moment and not on what happened in a previous shot or on what is going to happen in a shot to come. The great golfers are the ones who are able to move on from a bad shot and see their current shot as a fresh start.

I've seen players carry one bad shot early in the round with them in their minds and ruin an entire round because of this.

A bad shot must be seen in the light of its ability to force a correction. We learn the most through our mistakes, not our successes. And we grow the most in tough times. If you can get your head around this and see tough times as a chance for growth and deeper meaning, you will arm yourself with the most powerful mental weapon known to man—optimism.

PATIENCE

Gary Player
1

Patience and fortitude conquer all things.
—Ralph Waldo Emerson

1965 US OPEN:
BELLERIVE COUNTRY CLUB, MISSOURI

If you think the pressure you place on yourself is draining, it can be nothing compared with the pressure placed on you by others.

I had won three Majors. Pretty good going, you would think. But now it was no longer a case of "Gary Player has won three Majors" but rather "Which three Majors has Gary Player won?" The British Open, the Masters, the PGA Championship . . . and you can see exactly where this was going at the time.

The US Open. When will Gary Player win that one? And if I had to be completely honest, at the time it was even a case of some asking if I ever would.

Foreigners just didn't win the US Open in the modern era. Harry Vardon did it in 1900, becoming the first non-American to win. Ted Ray also achieved the feat in 1920. But it eluded South Africa's Bobby Locke, and he told me it was the one thing missing from his amazing career.

Of course, I wasn't immune to the aura of the US Open either. It had long been in my mind to win the US Open. But let's face it, American golfers dominated their national Open.

And of course, there was another not-so-small matter hanging in the balance here as well. The "Big Three"—the collective term for the dominance of Arnold Palmer, Jack Nicklaus, and me—was now an established fact in the game. Between us we have won nearly sixty Majors on both the PGA and senior (now Champions) tours. This has never happened before by any three players and may never happen again.

By 1965, each of us had won three of the four Majors in the game. For Arnold, the PGA Championship was proving the elusive title. For Jack, it was the British Open. And for me, the US Open. I'd come close in 1958, finishing as runner-up four strokes behind Tommy Bolt.

So it came to pass that on a sweltering week in Missouri, in what is considered one of the most searching and demanding tests of golf established by the United States Golf Association (USGA), the Grand Slam was beckoning. And for a foreigner on top of it.

As always, I did my homework. Ben Hogan was a master of the US Open, and he always arrived well before the tournament to get used to the local conditions. Like Hogan, I made sure I had my daily routine running smoothly, down to the finest detail. I didn't go out for dinner and stayed in my hotel room at night.

I'm not a superstitious person, but I washed my same black golf shirt after every round and wore the same outfit every day.

Then I studied the golf course. It was a monster. At 7,190 yards it was the longest of any US Open golf course in history at that time, and it was made even longer by the lousy equipment and balls we had. During the practice rounds, I made copious notes and sketches of the course and greens and would then study them in my hotel room in the evenings.

I started off well by shooting an opening round 70 and was two shots off the lead of Australian Kel Nagle. I added another 70 in the second round and led Nagle by one stroke. A 71 in the third round kept me in front. It came down to the final nine holes and what was now just a battle between Nagle and me. I was three strokes ahead of him to start the round.

Nagle played superbly over those closing holes, cutting my lead down to only one stroke before I again opened up a three-stroke lead with three holes to play.

I stepped onto the tee at the par-three 16th. It's a long hole, and I had a three wood in my hands. But then the wind died suddenly. I changed to a four wood, but in my mind I had this thought that I needed to hit it quickly before the next gust of wind came up again. It was a classic example of how impatience can cost you.

My ball finished in a plugged lie in the greenside bunker, and I made five. Nagle had made three, cutting my lead to one again. And when Nagle birdied the 17th, it vanished completely. We ended regulation play tied for the lead, setting up an eighteen-hole play-off on Monday.

I putted superbly in that play-off and was five up through the first eight holes on my way to winning the tournament with a 71 to Nagle's 74.

I had finally done it. I had won the US Open. I had won my first Major in a play-off. I had won the Grand Slam. I had become only the third person in history to win all four Majors, at the age of twenty-nine. I had followed in the footsteps of Gene Sarazen and Ben Hogan. And more significant, I was the first foreigner to accomplish the feat. Forty-five years later, I remain the only one to do so.

I was also the first of "The Big Three" to reach this milestone. I particularly wanted to beat Jack Nicklaus to winning the Grand Slam. And Jack was a great sport about it. He urged me to practice with him the week before this Major rather than play in another tournament in St Louis. I told him I couldn't because I needed the money from another tournament in Greensboro, North Carolina, but he persisted and played a part in my winning the Grand Slam before him.

From a young age, when I first turned professional, winning the Grand Slam was something I always wanted to achieve. I'd read about Sarazen and Hogan having done it and Bobby Jones winning his own amateur Grand Slam.

It was a great moment in my life, and I'm honored and grateful to have achieved it. No man does this on his own. It is merely a talent that is loaned to you. We have seen this talent taken away from many golfers whether permanently or for a while: Ian Baker-Finch, Tom Watson, David Duval, to name a few.

THE CHOKE CHALLENGE

Patience is vital when it comes to dealing with pressure. Jack Nicklaus once said that he always admired my patience. I've been a very patient person. I'm a great believer in what will be, will

be. You can't force the issue. In the 1965 US Open, I knew there were a lot of expectations on me to win that next Major, and the pressure to do so was palpable. It had been three years since my last Major triumph. But I knew the right time would come. I was still young and not even thirty yet.

And after all, your own expectations are all that matter.

The way I won was also important for me. I went to the scoreboard every day, and it had all the past champions listed there. And every day I visualized my name on that list. In the play-off, I kept telling myself, "You are twenty-nine and playing against a forty-four-year-old man. You're in excellent physical shape. Make it count."

An interesting aside to this Major is that when I was handed the winner's check, I gave it straight back to Joe Dey, who was then the director of the USGA, and asked him to donate it to cancer research in honor of my mother, who passed away as a result of this terrible disease, and to junior golf development.

I was fulfilling a promise I had made to Joe a few years earlier in 1962 on the last hole (the seventy-second) of the US Open at Oakmont in Pittsburgh. I told him that if I ever won the US Open, I would donate the prize money to these two causes.

There is enormous satisfaction in giving something back in moments of great success. My mother died of cancer when I was only eight years old, and I saw her suffer, so this was number one on my charity list. Because I suffered myself as a junior, young people became my number two charity.

MAJOR MENTALITY

If I had to name one enduring quality that all of the great golfers have had, it would be patience.

During regulation play on the par-three 16th in the 1965 US Open, my indecision about club selection postponed my victory and forced me into a play-off. But the true mistake was rushing that shot. The Chinese have a wonderful saying about patience: "Pick the flower when it is ready to be picked."

There is a big difference between patience and procrastination.

One involves just waiting. The other involves waiting for the right time to make your move. Patience, practiced correctly, is a powerful mental tool that unlocks so many other positives and that will also give you the kind of perspective others may lack under pressure. We have a simple saying, and we know it but don't adhere to it: "Patience is a virtue." What a dynamic saying.

IT AIN'T MEANT TO BE EASY

To struggle when hope is banished!
To live when life's salt is gone!
To dwell in a dream that's vanished—
To endure, and go calmly on!

—Ben Jonson

1968 BRITISH OPEN:
CARNOUSTIE, SCOTLAND

Let me tell you about Carnoustie.

As golfers we can all enjoy the beauty and challenge of a great course such as Augusta National. We can marvel at the antiquity and history embodied in the Old Course at St Andrews. And there are a host of golf courses worldwide that each possesses its own special charm. But there is nothing charming about Carnoustie. It is a bleak course in a bleak town. And I mean it no disrespect when I describe it as such. The people there are wonderful and make it such a great place to play. Carnoustie is harsh and most often cruel. It will take the slightest weakness in your game and tear it all to shreds.

Even Ben Hogan, when he first saw Carnoustie prior to the 1953 Open, thought he'd made a mistake going over there and was thinking about turning around and going back home. But whatever all the great golfers think of Carnoustie, one thing is clear—everybody respects it.

In 1968, Carnoustie was hosting its fourth Open Championship. It was set up as the longest course in Open history at 7,252 yards. From the start, Carnoustie presented a fierce challenge. The wind was brutal in the first round, and only four players managed to break par. I struggled to a two-over 74.

In those situations, it's very difficult to remain positive. The problem is often not your own thoughts but the thoughts of those around you. Everybody, from the players to the media, was talking about how tough Carnoustie was, how tough the weather was, and so on. It's hard to keep yourself positive when there is so much negativity around you. My saving grace was that I was able to always shut this negativity out and stay focused on the job at hand.

The two best bad-weather players I ever saw were Tom Watson and Arnold Palmer. The worse the conditions got, the better they played. I was like that when confronted with negativity. I just became more positive. My belief was that if it's bad for everybody, then make sure it's good for only you.

Some good putting helped me to a 71 in the second round, and another 71 on day three put me within two shots of the lead going into the final round.

"Viv, I just blew the Open Championship."

The first few holes on Sunday took an immediate toll, but I held on and took the lead for the first time on the 6th. By the 13th I was tied for the lead with Sir Bob Charles and Billy Casper, with my playing partner Jack Nicklaus two shots back and Maurice Bembridge right there too. The weather was tough, the course was in a foul mood, and some of the greatest golfers of their time were hovering around me just waiting for me to make a mistake.

I'd like to say it's easy playing a great shot when all the conditions are perfect. But the greatest shots are played when the odds are stacked against you. And the three wood that I hit for my second shot on the treacherous par-five 14th hole named the Spectacles, finishing inches from the flag, is probably the greatest shot I've ever hit in my life.

The reason is as I explained above. The conditions were terrible. So much so that Casper and Charles were starting to drop shots, and Nicklaus couldn't make anything happen himself.

It was an unbelievable shot, and I have no doubt that it won me this Open, as it propelled me toward the eagle that carried me to victory. My wife was in the stands, and she said it best: "My legs were like jelly climbing off of the stands."

THE CHOKE CHALLENGE

Carnoustie was not easy. Far from it. But come on! Major championships are not meant to be easy. The biggest challenges of your life are exactly that—the biggest. It's your final examination paper, and it's not supposed to be easy. So get rid of any idea that this should be easy. If it was, then you wouldn't be a great world champion by overcoming it. You'd just be good. Whether

MAJOR MENTALITY

When you sit down to take an exam, nobody gives you the answers. And when you set out to become the world's greatest golfer, athlete, or whatever, nobody hands it to you and says, "Don't worry about training for it." It's hard because it's so seldom achieved.

If all of us could play tennis like Roger Federer or Rod Laver, how would we know who the best in the world was? And how would we have something to aspire to?

So don't complain about how tough it is. Just accept that it's meant to be tough. Otherwise it wouldn't be as special when you achieve it.

Life is about challenging yourself, not finding the easy way out.

It's only through constantly challenging yourself that you will learn more about who you are and what you can become.

A young Scot playing with his dad said, "Dad, your ball is in the rough, and what a perfect lie. My ball is in the middle of the fairway, and I am in a deep divot; that's not fair."

"Son," the father replied, "the game ain't meant to be fair." Is that not indicative of life itself?

the course is tough, the greens are bad, the weather is cold, or whatever it is, just accept that this is the challenge that has been placed before you and tackle it. No amount of moaning is going to make it any easier.

DON'T BE AFRAID TO GO FOR IT 1

> Men were born to succeed, not to fail.
>
> —Henry David Thoreau

1972 PGA CHAMPIONSHIP:
OAKLAND HILLS COUNTRY CLUB, MICHIGAN

Ben Hogan said the secret to his great golf was in the dirt; my secret to winning this Major was in a divot.

Memory is incredibly important in Major championship golf, and a particular memory played a big part in my sixth Major title.

During the practice round, I hit an eight iron for my second shot from right of the fairway on the 16th at Oakland Hills. After I hit the shot, for some strange reason the divot caught my attention. "That's a funny-looking divot," I thought to myself.

Then came the final round. There were ten of us within two shots of each other and the lead playing the final nine holes. With a one-shot lead, I teed off on the 16th and hit my drive into the right rough. When I reached my ball, I was a bit concerned. I'd bogeyed holes 14 and 15, and now I was in the rough with this big willow tree in front of me and water guarding the green.

I had worked incredibly hard for this Major, and now I felt it was slipping away from me. This is a dangerous place to be in mentality, and it's here where choking becomes a factor. Once I'd reached my ball, I started working out my yardages and so on. I was walking to a marker on the fairway, and that's when I saw it. The same divot I had made in the practice round was still there.

I knew immediately that the shot I had from the rough would be a nine iron. I'd hit an eight in the practice round, and although I was in a similar position, the grass was wet now, and I knew I would get a bit of a flyer coming out of that rough. It was 150 yards, and I hit that nine iron perfectly. It sailed over the willow tree and onto the green, finishing three feet from the hole. It was an amazing shot, and it secured me the birdie that I needed to win the tournament by two shots over Tommy Aaron and Jim Jamieson.

I've hit some incredible shots in my career, and people often thought I was just lucky. But great shots, much like great championship victories, are often the result of careful planning and something that gives you that courage and conviction deep inside to know you can pull it off. Great shots don't simply appear out of nowhere during a crucial stage of a Major. They are shots that have been grooved on the practice range for hours. What makes them special is the player's ability to execute the shot under pressure.

That's the secret. And for me, the secret to this one was in that divot.

THE CHOKE CHALLENGE

This was a classic case of taking a gamble when the time was right. Oakland Hills was a monster of a golf course. Even before the Major started, I said that it was the toughest course in America. With modern-day equipment it would not have been.

Ben Hogan, scoring a final round 67 to win the US Open one year, was quoted saying, "I have tamed the monster."

There were precious few opportunities to take anything away from this course, and you had to choose those moments wisely. Knowing when to take a risk comes from experience. You need to know your own game and capabilities. Throughout my career, if I had any doubt as to whether or not I could reach a green in two, I'd lay up because I knew I was going to be putting for a birdie. I knew I was a good wedge player and putter and that there were few players who holed more putts than me inside of ten feet. But if I hit it in the water, I would be in big trouble. So you need to know and understand your game. You've almost got to fool yourself and say, "Well, if I lay up, I'm definitely going to make a four." Not maybe. Definitely. That's positive thinking in a practical sense. It's a case of knowing the strengths of your game and then visualizing success based on those strengths.

But there are times to take a risk and times to play safe. Look at the case of Jean Van de Velde in the 1999 British Open at Carnoustie. When I had a two-shot lead playing the last hole there in 1968, I hit a three iron, a four iron, and then a nine iron onto the green. With a three-shot lead, Van de Velde hit a driver, which he was unlucky not to put in the water. If the shot had gone in the water, he would've won, because then he would've dropped out and played short for three, on for four, and taken a six and the title. But instead the ball bounced favorably, or unfavorably in the end, and left him with a good lie. And he decided to go for the green. Why? There is out of bounds on the left, grandstands on the right, and water in front. Why are you going for it? If you've got a three-shot lead on such a demanding final hole, you take a five iron, a six iron, and a wedge, and you make a bogey

The willow tree shot.

and you win. But he decided to go for it, and the ball hit the grandstands and bounced in the water. And everybody said he was unlucky. But what do you think is supposed to happen—you hit the stands and bounce onto the pin?

Take the risk, but know the strengths of your game to make sure you're not just hitting and hoping. That's the difference between taking a risk and the simple blind ignorance that is merely hoping for a positive outcome. Jack Nicklaus or Tiger Woods would never have made this mistake. Tiger once hit a three iron off the tee at Doral needing a bogey to win.

MAJOR MENTALITY

I have made many decisions in my life, and some have been good and others bad. But I have never regretted making a decision. I'd rather make a decision and stick with it than not make a decision and be racked with uncertainty. If you feel the time is right, then go for it. Don't second-guess yourself. Go for it with all you have and commit. And if it doesn't come off, then so be it. Accept it as such and move on. But keep making decisions. Jack Nicklaus won eighteen Majors, but he also finished second in nineteen others.

Jack was certainly not the hardest worker I ever saw, but he was not lazy though. If Jack had ever thought Tiger or any other golfer would match or surpass him, he would have worked and prepared harder and have won at least three to five more majors. I have no doubt about this. You simply cannot compare Woods and Nicklaus with times and equipment being so different. It is like comparing oranges and bananas.

Accept it as such and move on. But keep making decisions.

Gary Player

WORK HARD, THEN EXPECT IT TO HAPPEN

Great works are performed not by strength,
but by perseverance.

—Samuel Johnson

1974 MASTERS:
AUGUSTA NATIONAL GOLF CLUB, GEORGIA

When I was a young boy, and I made up my mind that I was going to be a world champion, I decided right there that I would practice harder than any human being who had ever played golf. I told my father, before I had even matriculated, that I was going to turn professional. I remember how he looked at me with great concern, and said, "You can't do that. I promised your mother before she died that you would go to university. How are you going to do it?" And I told him, "Don't worry, I will do it." I was going to work harder than anybody to get there. Practice and sheer hard work were going to be my paths to success.

I was an animal with regard to practice. I have always said that there is no such thing as a natural golfer. The sixteen months it took me to go from first picking up a golf club to a scratch golfer was through very little amount of natural ability and had more to do with the hours I spent practicing. I've seen players with all the talent in the world not amount to anything because they didn't work hard enough. Ben Hogan once said that there are not enough hours in the day for all the shots he needed to practice to become a champion. I played with him in the 1958 US Open, when I finished second. Afterward, in the locker room, Hogan came up to me and said, "Well played. Do you practice hard?" I felt like saying, "Just as hard as you sir," but with respect I merely answered, "Yes sir." He replied, "Double it" and went into the dining room. Practice helps to strengthen your mind.

I traveled to Augusta National in 1974 with a firm belief that I was going to win because I knew I had worked harder than anybody else there. My confidence was at an incredible high, and it showed.

In the third round I scored a 66, including five straight birdies from the 12th hole. And on the 17th green on the final day, I hit a nine iron and knew immediately that it was going to be something special. I even turned to my caddie as soon as I'd hit it and said, "We're not going to putt this one." I believed it was headed straight for the hole. Instead, it finished eight inches short.

Throughout my career there were periods where I entered this state of self-hypnosis during a round of golf, and this was a classic example thereof.

I remember playing in a tournament in South Africa, with my family watching from the gallery. One of my racehorses, Welcome Boy, had just won a major race. As I was walking down the fairway, my son, Marc, called out to me and said, "Dad, your horse won." I gave him the filthiest look. I was so focused at that time that I didn't want anything to break that concentration.

Practice gives you the confidence to get into that state of mind and stay there.

I used meditation and self-hypnosis throughout my career and still do. Self-hypnosis is a big thing of the future and should be looked at as beneficial, not as a thing that hippies or tree huggers do because they are "so out there." The mind, not raw ability and skill, plays the most important role in success.

THE CHOKE CHALLENGE

There are people who dream of doing well but do nothing to fulfill that dream. It takes sacrifice to fulfill-that dream. Success requires a massive sacrifice, in one way or another. You are the only one who can make that dream happen. Nobody is going to do it for you. You need to work for everything that you get, because when it comes too easily, you don't appreciate it.

So get out there and work for it. Work for it when you don't feel like working for it. Whenever you do something that you don't want to do or don't feel like doing, it builds a strength of mind that nobody can take away from you. It's this strength of mind that shines through when the chips are down.

They say, "Be careful what you wish for, you just might get it."

I say, "Be careful what you work hard for, because you will get it."

MAJOR MENTALITY

"The harder I practice, the luckier I get" is a saying people have heard from me all my life. But one of the ten commandments I drew up for myself early in my life, which is the cornerstone of our business philosophy, says: "The fox fears not the man who boasts by night but the man who rises early in the morning."

There is no substitute for hard work. There are no shortcuts. You can't play a par five in only one shot. There are dreamers, and there are doers.

Winston Churchill said, "The heights by great men reached and kept, were not attained by sudden flight, but they, while their companions slept, were toiling upward in the night." I did this a lot in my life. Getting the key from a hotel manager to use the gym when I got back late from a dinner engagement rather than going to bed is just one example. I knew that if I worked harder than everyone else, I would win, and I did.

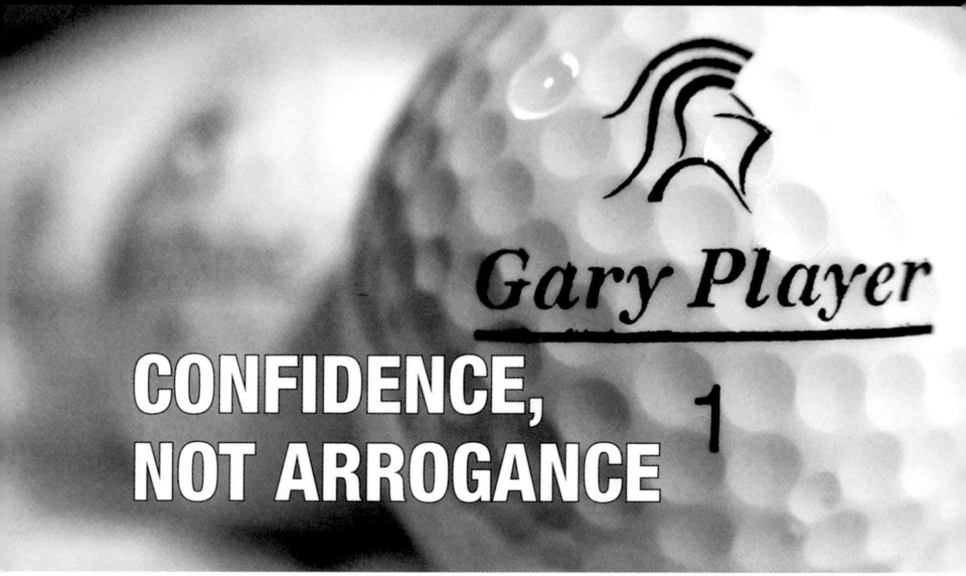

CONFIDENCE, NOT ARROGANCE

1

To become truly great, one has to stand with people,
not above them.

—Charles de Montesquieu

1974 BRITISH OPEN:
ROYAL LYTHAM & ST ANNES, ENGLAND

Perfection in golf is obviously very hard to attain, but I must say I felt like I came close to it at Lytham in 1974. I led the Open that year from start to finish, playing some of the best golf of my life. I opened with a 69 and followed it up with a 68 to be five strokes clear of the field at the halfway mark. And until the final round, there wasn't another golfer in that field able to break 70.

The wind was typically tough that week. It really got hold of me in the third round, and I struggled to a 75. But I was still three

Left-handed shot against wall.

shots ahead of the rest of the field, led by Peter Oosterhuis, when I teed off on the final day.

There was some drama on that final day, but fortunately at that stage I held a six-shot lead with two holes to play. I nearly

suffered a lost ball on 17 and found my second shot in the deep
rough with only a few seconds of allowable time to spare. I was
only five yards off the green, but I hooked my second shot, and
the marshal said it bounced off the edge of the green into the
thick rough.

And then at the last hole, I hit my second shot over the green,
and it came to rest alongside the clubhouse wall, forcing me to
play back to the green left-handed.

But overall I felt as in control of my game that week as I ever have. I was confident in my own ability and my golf game, so much so that I never allowed people's opinions to sway me, because that's when you open the door to choking.

The wind was blowing gales that week, the fairways were narrow, and I went around that course with a one iron. Most of the golfers at that time said, "You can't win the British Open with a one iron," but I never listened to them. I had done my homework and knew that in that wind, a one iron was the best club for me to use to keep the ball low and get the most run on it. The result is that I had a six-shot lead with two holes to go and won the tournament.

My confidence was on another level entirely in 1974.

With this victory I became only the second player since Harry Vardon—and the first in the twentieth century—to win the Open Championship in three separate decades, following my victories at Muirfield in '59 and Carnoustie in '68. I am very proud of this achievement. Money does not define your life or your success. Achievements do. The fact that you can be the best in the world is something unique.

But success doesn't give you the right to think you are more important than anybody else. Instead, it should give you the right to realize that you are blessed.

THE CHOKE CHALLENGE

You can be confident without being arrogant. There is a humility about true confidence, a humility to say, "I'm going to work as hard as I can and put everything into this," which in turn breeds the confidence to achieve. Arrogance lacks this very

important foundation. Arrogance says, "I'm great just because I am." Confidence says, "I'm great because I've worked so hard to become who I am." There is a fine line between confidence and arrogance. Jealous people always have their translations.

MAJOR MENTALITY

Thomas Carlyle wrote of a "nobleness" and "sacredness" in work. Treat it as such, particularly when it comes to your relationship with others. There is no substitute for personal contact. Arrogance is very self-centered, and when you are self-centered, there is no room for growth. Confidence is a belief in your own ability without a belief in the inferiority of others.

1974 Brazillian Open

SHOOTING 59

In 1974 I traveled to Brazil to compete in the Brazilian Open against a good international field. I was determined to win the tournament and played very well. What I was not expecting was the final round that I put together. I bogeyed one hole on the front nine and moved to the back with the championship in sight. The birdies came like rain, and on the final hole I was faced with a putt to card the first ever 59 in tournament play. I made the putt. During the round, and especially on the back nine, I was completely relaxed and actually enjoying the pressure. I was reveling in it. My mind, much more than my skill, is what allowed me to shoot a 59.

Fifty-nine was like a mental block in the golf world, very similar to what the four-minute mile was to the track and field world. When Roger Bannister broke the four-minute mark, it was historic not only because it was the first time it had ever been done but also because it ended the belief that the four-minute mile was impossible. What few know is that within one year of Bannister breaking the mark, college students did the same. People believed that it could be done and then did it. It was the same thing with 59. The psychological hurdle of breaking 60 was gone.

The lesson here is to believe that you can do something that seems impossible. I did not set out to shoot 59, but I never doubted that I could do it. When the chance presented itself, I did it.

ENTHUSIASM HAS[1] NO AGE LIMIT

> Blessed is he who has found his work.
>
> —Thomas Carlyle

1978 MASTERS:
AUGUSTA NATIONAL GOLF CLUB, GEORGIA

I was seven strokes off the lead at the start of the final round of the 1978 Masters. But everything that was to be in this particular Masters was born in the late hours of a night earlier in the week.

I had left the Champions dinner on Tuesday night at 10 PM. At the age of forty-two and with eight Major championships behind my name, I could have gone straight to bed. But I didn't. I went straight to the gym and forced myself to fit in my daily exercise program.

When I started exercising religiously while on tour, people said I would never last as a golfer. They said you couldn't train with weights and be a champion in golf. They spoke of losing your touch and a lot of other rubbish.

When I was advocating certain concepts about fitness and nutrition, they all said I was crazy. But today, a lot of pros train hard on tour. In fact, now they even have a traveling gym on most tours. But back then, you had to go and knock on the hotel manager's door late at night and ask him to please open up the gym for you so you could train, or you made a trip to the local YMCA.

I didn't want to be in the gym at that time of night. I could have told myself I was tired and needed the rest. I hear a lot of professional golfers today who say they are tired after they have played for three weeks in a row. These golfers are playing for millions of dollars, for money the average man on the street won't see in his entire lifetime. And he has to hear how tired they are.

The average factory worker doesn't have the luxury of working three weeks and then taking two weeks off. He works like a Trojan for two weeks off all year, if he's lucky. My father worked at the bottom of a gold mine until he was drenched in sweat. He couldn't say he was tired. If he choked in a pressure situation, he wouldn't get paid. Or worse, it could've cost him his life. Imagine what the average man thinks when he hears pros say that they are tired? I always kept this in mind, and the fact that I knew that working while my opponents were sleeping would give me an advantage.

Usually, the people who attain the most success are the ones putting in the most effort.

So I went to that gym and worked as hard as I had done throughout my career and continue to work to this day. And that week I became the oldest winner of the Masters. I walked out

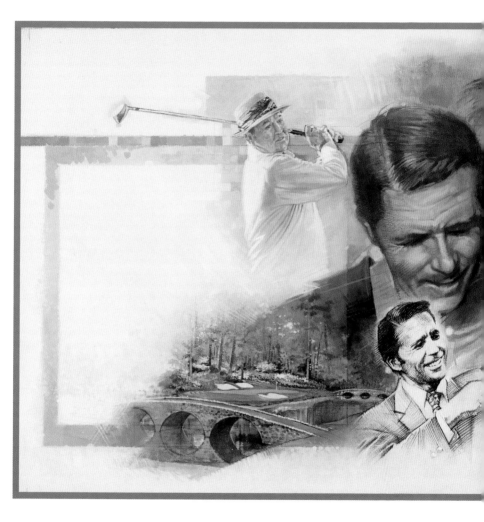

of that gym and to a final round of eight-under-par 64. I did it by shooting 30 for the final nine holes. That back nine has gone down as one of the finest in the history of the Masters. Indeed it is one of the finest in Major championship golf. I'm thankful for that recognition.

On the 10th I hit a five iron to thirty-five feet and made the putt for birdie. On the 12th I hit a seven iron to fifteen feet and made the birdie. On the 13th I hit a four iron with everything I had and two-putted for birdie. On the 15th, a three wood put me eighty feet from the hole, and I two-putted for a birdie. On 16 I holed a twenty-footer for birdie. And on the last hole, I hit a six iron into the green and holed another twenty-footer for birdie.

I was very flattered by a report of this round written by the great golf writer Herbert Warren Wind in which he said, "I very much doubt if anyone with a chance to win has ever played the last nine holes of a Major Championship as well as Player did the last nine of the 1978 Masters."

THE CHOKE CHALLENGE

Enthusiasm is one of the greatest essences of life. People often criticized me in my career when I said, "That was the best shot of my life" or "That was the best round of my life." They said, "That Gary Player always says that." But I was always so in the moment during a Major that I truly believed it. And I had brainwashed myself to be enthusiastic about everything good in my game and to keep building my own confidence. That enthusiasm is what carried me from the golf course to the gym to keep working hard at getting better.

Remember, nobody else will ever be as enthusiastic about you as you. Don't associate with people who are miserable and negative.

MAJOR MENTALITY

It's often said that if a golfer's mind is somewhere else while he is playing, it will show up most clearly in his putting. Focus a hundred percent on what you are busy with. Immerse yourself in it and do it with enthusiasm. Love what you are busy with. This is your time, and it's going to be as good as you want it to be. Nobody else and nothing else can make you enthusiastic about your life. Only you. William Pierson Merrill said, "Expect the best." And the apostle Paul, while he was locked up in a dungeon with the threat of execution hanging over him, was still able to write that in all situations he had learned to be content and happy with life, because of that inde-structible enthusiasm he had about doing God's work. Be happy and make the most of your life.

Gary Player

THE OLD PEAR TREE 1

I t was an old pear tree, and it stood at the back of our house in Booysens, a working-class suburb in Johannesburg, South Africa. In a suburb where most of the men, like my father, worked in the gold mines and the huge mountains of sand they dug out of the earth dotted the landscape, the old pear tree stood like a green beacon to us.

So we did what young boys do—we set about conquering it. My older brother Ian and I hung a rope from one of its huge branches, and we'd climb up and down it almost every day.

Soon, it became competitive, and we challenged each other. If Ian managed to climb up and down that rope four times, then I did it five times.

We moved in 1947. About fifteen years later, I stood in front of that house again. I was back in South Africa for a brief time and thought I'd make a sentimental pilgrimage back to the family house. I walked out to the backyard, and there stood the old pear tree. And hanging from it was that rope.

I cut it down and took it with me, the memory of my brother giving me ten cents to do it one more time still fresh in my mind.

I have often thought back to the significance of that rope. It was there, in that backyard, in a suburb very much on the wrong side of the tracks, that I first started climbing. I climbed to the top of my game in South Africa. Then I climbed to the top of the world. And then, in November 1985, I reached the milestone of fifty years of age. Many people have a mental cutoff in terms of their personal and business growth. Once they reach fifty, they start thinking about "winding down" to retirement. I looked down at a pair of hands that were calloused from the "climbing" they had done. They had conquered everything there was to conquer in the game of golf. And still, it wasn't enough.

So I tied that rope to a new branch—that of the Champions Tour (then called the Senior PGA Tour) and the game of business. If I could win nine Majors on the regular tour, then why, I argued, could I not win nine Majors on the Champions Tour as well?

It felt good to feel that rope in my hands again. The hands were not those of a boy. They were more wrinkled. But they hadn't forgotten.

You never stop climbing.

Today I have the most Majors, nine, on the Champions Tour. Jack Nicklaus has eight, and Tom Watson and Arnold Palmer each have five. Strength is not what gives you success; it is perseverance.

REVIRESCO

*R*eviresco is an interesting word that held special meaning for me during my career and life. It is Latin in origin and means to grow green again, to grow strong or young again.

My mental approach to the game and life can be defined by this word alone. As I have mentioned many times throughout the book, when you make a mistake, fail, or do not perform to the best of your abilities, doubt and indecision start to creep into your mind. The ability to manage, overcome, and learn from these experiences is what separates the good from the great. It enabled me to overcome adversity and succeed, not only in golf but in life. If I had let those negative thoughts take root in my brain, I would have failed.

I always thought of reviresco when I failed, choked, or made a mistake. I knew that I would grow stronger with every setback. I would grow green again.

When I began my career on the Champions Tour, reviresco took on an additional meaning, the literal one—to grow green again, to grow strong or young again. I was fifty, in excellent physical and mental health, and ready to begin the next stage of my career. I knew that my window to win was now significantly shorter than it was on the PGA Tour. I figured that I had maybe five to ten years to complete my next and possibly my most satisfying career goal—the career Grand Slam on the Champions Tour.

Here is how I did it.

THE
BACK
NINE

PART II

THE SENIOR SLAM

G ary launched into his remarkable Senior career as soon as he became eligible at age 50 in November 1985. He entered his first Senior event within three weeks of his birthday and, in characteristic Player fashion, came from behind to win the event – the Quadel Senior Classic – by three strokes!

One of Gary's rare achievements is to have secured the Grand Slam "double" – winning the four Majors in both the regular tours as well as the Seniors. And he has done it in style, with three British Senior Open titles (1988, 1990 and 1997); three US Senior PGA titles (1986, 1988 and 1990); two US Senior Open titles (1987 and 1988); and one US Senior Tournament Players Championship title (1987).

When he won the British Senior Open in 1997, it gave him his ninth "Major" title as a Senior, matching his nine "Majors" on the regular tours.

LET YOUR YESTERDAYS BUILD YOUR TOMORROWS

Gary Player

> A successful man is one who can lay a firm foundation with the bricks others have thrown at him.
>
> —David Brinkley

1986 SENIOR PGA CHAMPIONSHIP:
PGA NATIONAL GOLF CLUB, FLORIDA

Winning the Grand Slam when you're in your twenties is obviously a great achievement. But let me tell you, winning the Grand Slam when you're over fifty and, as they say, your back goes out more than you do is more of an achievement in my book.

I've always felt that my Grand Slam on the senior tour was far greater an achievement than my Grand Slam on the regular tour. The most obvious reason for this is that I was older, having turned fifty in November 1985. It's natural that as you get older,

your nerve tends to weaken. Yet here I was, setting myself up for a new challenge, having to make sure that the same desire and competitive instinct that fueled me in my younger years would last until the age of sixty.

Then there was also the challenge of playing against some of the greatest champions in the game. Many people are unaware of just how competitive the Champions Tour is. The scoring is often as impressive as any regular tour event, and many Champions Tour players were still winning on the regular tour. In my first year on the Champions Tour, the scoring average was 69. That's a good average in any golfer's book. In fact, the year before I joined the tour, Don January and Jimmy Powell had set scoring records such as recording three eagles in one round, and Peter Thomson won nine tournaments that year.

Don was a tremendous force on the Champions Tour, topping the money list in 1980, 1983, and 1984. In 1986, Australia's Bruce Crampton was the foremost player on the tour. He won seven tournaments that year.

And of course I also had my longtime opponents such as Arnold Palmer, Lee Trevino, and later Jack Nicklaus and Tom Watson to compete against. For goodness' sake, in 1986 and at the age of forty-six, Nicklaus was still teaching them a thing or two on the regular tour when he won the Masters that year. So relatively speaking, my time on the Champions Tour was as competitive as any other time in my career.

The golf courses were also of the highest quality. PGA National Golf Club is a remarkable facility with five golf courses that between them have hosted over twenty Major championships and the Ryder Cup. The Champion Course is the jewel in this collection. It hosted the 1983 Ryder Cup and the 1987 PGA Championship and had become the permanent home of the

Senior PGA Championship. It's a very challenging layout and at one stage was ranked as the ninth most difficult course on the PGA Tour. The closing stretch of holes 15 to 17 is incredibly demanding. Holes 15 and 17 are par threes played over water, and hole 16 is a tough par four with an approach over water. So true to the golf course's name, you need to produce champion shots to win on it.

But the passion that fueled me on the regular tour was still there, and I quickly set about refocusing my goals and facing up to this new challenge. Most important, I had experience on my side. I was a nine-time Major champion on the regular tour and a multiple tournament winner worldwide. I was a successful businessman and a successful father. And while age may mean you don't hit the ball as far anymore, it doesn't mean you have stopped knowing how to win.

Once I had made that mental shift in my head and adjusted to a new chapter in my life, I set about achieving these new goals.

In my third start on the Champions Tour, I beat Lee Elder by two stokes to become only the third foreigner after Thomson (1984) and Argentina's Roberto De Vicenzo (1974) to win the Senior PGA Championship. This was particularly pleasing because the Senior PGA Championship has such a proud history dating back to 1937.

A new desire to be a world champion in a different time in my life had been born.

THE CHOKE CHALLENGE

The key to longevity in business or a career is a solid foundation. The fact that I was so fit gave me a big advantage to win nine Majors on the Champions Tour.

I arrived on the senior tour with a solid base. This meant that although I may have faced a few different challenges in the sense that physically I was not the same golfer I was in my youth, I still had an incredible base to draw from in terms of experience. It's this kind of base that allows you to refocus very quickly and adapt to a new environment. It enables you to overcome whatever different challenges you may face in your new environment and draw on the mental strength of past experience to shape your future goals.

Both Ben Hogan and Bobby Locke had their five fundamentals that they believed were critical to achieving success in the game of golf. These fundamentals formed the base on which they built their games and careers. The fundamentals that make up the foundation of your business or career are what will allow you to continually refocus and adapt to new challenges.

Keep reevaluating your fundamentals and make sure that the foundation you have built remains firm. You can call them your life lessons, business commandments, or whatever seems appropriate to you.

I have developed my own set of commandments that I have tried to live my life by, and I have made them the foundation of my business and personal life.

They are as follows:

1. Change is the price of survival.
2. Everything in business is negotiable except quality.
3. A promise made is a debt incurred.
4. For all we take in life we must pay.
5. Persistence and common sense are more important than intelligence.
6. The fox fears not the man who boasts by night but the man who rises early in the morning.

7. Accept the advice of those who love you, though you like it not at present.

8. Trust instinct to the end, though you cannot render any reason.

9. The heights by great men reached and kept were not attained by sudden flight, but they, while their companions slept, were toiling upward in the night.

10. There is no substitute for personal contact.

As long as your foundation is strong, you can build into any new area of your life you wish.

MAJOR MENTALITY

Fundamentals. Consider what your career has been built on. Make a note of the fundamentals that you believe to be important. It's these fundamentals that will shape your success in business.

When I began to shift focus from my playing career to my business career, I had certain fundamentals that I wasn't willing to compromise on. For example, I have always stated that in business, everything is negotiable except quality. These were fundamentals that I also applied to my playing career on the regular tour. They built my success on the golf course, and they helped build my success in business.

The strength of your foundation determines the heights of your success.

Gary Player

COMPLACENCY BREEDS CHOKING [1]

Follow your passion, and success will follow you.
—**Arthur Buddhold**

1987 SENIOR TPC:
SAWGRASS COUNTRY CLUB, FLORIDA

I was extremely frustrated.

I arrived at Sawgrass not having won in quite some time, and I didn't like it one bit. Those old feelings of not performing to the best of my ability were haunting me just as they had done throughout my younger years.

I could quite easily have told myself that my past successes justified at least one mediocre year. But having set myself the new goal of winning the Grand Slam on the senior tour, I can honestly tell you that I didn't give a damn about what I'd won last week, never mind last year. Now I was driven to be the best on the Champions Tour, and every week that went by where I didn't play to this level was a tremendous frustration to me.

At Sawgrass, as had been the case for pretty much this whole year, Chi Chi Rodriguez was the man to beat. Rodriguez was playing unbelievably good golf, and he was hunting his fifth consecutive victory on the Champions Tour. He'd also won the Senior PGA Championship earlier in the year. And when he opened with a 65, there were many who were willing to give him the tournament right there.

I could just as easily have written off my chances and played for the security of a moderate level of success in this Major. But I did not make the sacrifices I have throughout my life just to be mediocre. Instead, I fought my way into contention on a Sawgrass course that was ferocious and that has always been a great leveler. The 1977 Tournament Players Championship was perhaps the best and most memorable example of what this course could do to some of the greatest players in the game. They dubbed the second round "Black Friday" for the scores that were recorded in tough, windy conditions on an unforgiving layout.

I finished tied for 13th in that tournament with scores of 74, 79, 71, and 72 for a total of eight over par. Arnold Palmer shot 78, 75, 74, and 75 that week, and Mark Hayes won the tournament with a total of one over par. If golf ever required an age restriction, then that Friday in 1977 would have been it. So this was no pushover of a golf course.

After working my way into contention, the championship eventually became a three-horse race between myself, Rodriguez, and Bruce Crampton. Our battle on this great golf course went all the way to the final hole, and I stood over an eight-foot birdie putt for the title.

Now, I was often a very aggressive player, and I took my chances when they came. But when it came to putting, I learned early in my career that charging a putt at the hole is the surest way to lose tournaments.

Bobby Locke was one of the finest putters the game has ever seen. Locke's philosophy on putting was that it is always better to leave a putt a little bit short than run it past the hole.

It is completely contrary to what you always hear. As golfers, we are taught from an early age to never leave a putt short. Sayings such as "Never up, never in" or "The hole won't come to you" are drilled into us. It's almost as if it's shameful to leave a putt short of the hole. But I've never seen one that goes past the hole go in either. And frankly, I'd rather be a few inches short of the hole than three feet past it.

Locke's reasoning was that if you hit a putt at just the right speed, it can drop in anywhere in the front of the hole, on the side or even at the back. But if you hit a putt hard, there's only one place it can go in, and that's in the center of the hole.

Throughout my career I've discovered that for every putt you charge at the hole, you sink ten putts with the right speed. Experience had taught me to be patient on the greens.

I holed that eight-foot birdie putt, and the title was mine by one stroke over Crampton and Rodriguez. But more important, I was now halfway to my senior Grand Slam in only my second year on the Champions Tour.

THE CHOKE CHALLENGE

You have to stay hungry. No matter how much success you have achieved in your career, you have to keep wanting to improve. There is no end to what we can achieve, and the only limitations that exist are the ones we place on ourselves.

If somebody had said to me when I was twenty that I could be the only person to win the Grand Slam on the regular tour and the senior tour, but I would die at fifty-five, I would've said, "You've got a deal." But now I realize that would've been crazy, as there would have been so many goals I would have missed out on achieving.

You can't afford to be complacent, because complacency breeds choking. The soft living that we enjoy these days is a big reason for the complacency that creeps into our lives. Maybe you have reached a point of success in your life where you say to yourself, "I've got a good life, and I deserve to rest on my laurels a bit." But in this life, what you deserve doesn't always translate into what you get. As much as you may feel like you deserve a break, the only breaks you get are the ones you make happen.

Keep setting goals. At any stage of your career, you've always got to have that goal that keeps your mind sharp and your spirit young. It's important to realize that you go through different stages in your career. So there is no point comparing your achievements. What is important is that you always reevaluate what you want to achieve and achieve success relative to the time you are in now.

MAJOR MENTALITY

Success is there to motivate us, not to keep us stagnant. Keep following your passion. You were not created to live a mediocre, safe life. You were created to bring into this world something unique and to leave it with an indelible impression that you gave it your all and made a difference.

Throw yourself into your passion and make sure it keeps driving you to new goals and greater achievements.

In your business environment, every day should be another opportunity for you to live out your passion and find new and exciting ways to make your mark.

EMBRACE
THE CHALLENGE

Gary Player

1

Citius, altius, fortius. (Swifter, higher, stronger.)
—Father Henri Martin Didon

1987 US SENIOR OPEN:
BROOKLAWN COUNTRY CLUB, CONNECTICUT

I've always believed in continually reevaluating my life and career and setting new goals for particular stages therein. When you train yourself to get fit, you don't train yourself just for a certain age or a certain time in your life. Your aim should be to train yourself to be fit for your whole life.

Life remains a challenge from Day One until the day you die. And it's a process of improving yourself as you go along. How many highly successful businesspeople go back to university at late stages in their lives to study something completely different and improve themselves in other areas? After all, we go to our graves knowing so little, and there is so much to learn.

At the age of fifty-two, I had my goals for this different time in my life.

I still regard the 1987 US Senior Open as one of my finest Major performances ever. A 69 in the first round was a good start, but it wasn't good enough for the lead. Gordon Jones and Peter Thomson both posted 66, then the lowest first round score to lead the US Senior Open. Jones's first round included an amazing run of scoring, with seven birdies in eight holes.

Chi Chi Rodriguez took the thirty-six-hole lead with a second-day 68, and I was still in the hunt only one shot behind him with a 68 of my own. Arnold Palmer was also a threat at two strokes off the lead.

I made my move late in the third round. The 415-yard par-four 17th at Brooklawn is a great hole. The green is protected by trees, mounds, and bunkers, and an aggressive approach is most likely to cost you a shot. Par is considered a good score there.

But as was the case throughout most of my career, I knew when to hold back and when to go for it. I took on the challenge and made a good birdie to catch Rodriguez for the first time in this Major. And when Rodriguez bogeyed the 18th, I had the lead on my own.

With victory in sight, I was as determined as ever to follow through in the final round. I started the round with four birdies in my first eight holes, and that gave me a four-stroke lead. With years of Major experience behind me, my mind was perfectly attuned to what was needed to close out this championship with a win.

A closing 66 gave me victory with a total of 270. It was a US Senior Open record, eclipsing the previous lowest total of 279 set by Dale Douglass the year before. My six-stroke victory was the

largest in US Senior Open history. I had also become the only
player to shoot all four rounds in the 60s, and it wasn't until 1995
that someone matched this feat—Tom Weiskopf.

I had also become the third man—after Arnold Palmer and
Billy Casper—to win both the US Open and US Senior Open.
And I was the second foreigner to win, following Argentinean
Roberto De Vicenzo, who won it in 1980. Carding 69, 68, 67,
and 66 gave me a special thrill. I just loved going one better each
day.

THE CHOKE CHALLENGE

Energy is one of the greatest gifts of life.

I have always spoken a lot about the value of fitness and nutrition. That has been the backbone of my life as a competitor at the highest level in the game and my success in other spheres as well. But few people ever speak about energy.

In my senior career, I can't believe the energy I still have.

You see, when you have all the comforts in the world, as most people do when they reach a certain age or stage in their careers, it is very easy to become if not physically obese then mentally obese.

Physical obesity definitely affects your mind and your ability to handle pressure because the blood circulation through your body is not that good. You may have all the experience in the world, but if you are faced against someone with less experience but in a better physical condition, I'm willing to say that you will be outdone by the more physically fit person. He may not be as brilliant at the time at making decisions in pressure situations, but over a span of time, he will have the energy to become better. And I've seen people in all walks of life with great energy.

I remember during my time on the regular tour, I arrived at the 1978 Masters in good form. My caddie for that week was Eddie McCoy. He came to greet me, and his arms were out, and he said, "Hey Gary, I need a house, man." I started laughing, and I said to him, "Eddie, we all need houses."

And he said, "But Gary, I really need a house. My family and I live in a crummy place," and he started to laugh again before adding even louder, "I need a house."

I laughed so much, and I said to him, "Well, Eddie, I'm playing well, so you've got a good chance of getting that house."

My son Wayne said to me, "Dad, you are playing so well, if you putt well you could shoot a 65 and win."

During that tournament, I never in all my life saw a caddie who was so nervous. When I was seven shots behind with one round to play, he wasn't feeling too confident about getting that house. Then I played the front nine in 34 on the final day, and Eddie was feeling a lot better about the situation. He was getting a little bit encouraged and could start to see a few windows going up in his house.

Then I started making all those birdies in that memorable back nine of 30, and all the way Eddie was like a cat on a hot tin roof. With every birdie I made he could see the roof going on, new doors being put in. When I holed the final birdie putt on 18, Eddie jumped from the side of the green like a grasshopper. He hugged me and thanked me for his house.

And my playing partner, Seve Ballesteros, walked over to me and said, "Gary, you teach me how to win Masters."

But Eddie walked off that 18th green so happy, it was like he had just become the Masters champion. He had a wonderful energy about him, and it worked for both of us that week.

MAJOR MENTALITY

Success in any career requires a measure of adaptability. And if you want the longevity you need in a successful career, you have to have the energy to see it through. Eating correctly gives you that extra energy.

All of this allows you to remain relevant throughout your business life. It gives you the tools to take your same game to a different course in a different time and still become a champion.

I thank God every day of my life for the amazing energy he has blessed me with. You have this same energy within you. Stop smothering it with the memory of past defeats or failures. Let your energy absolutely crush any negative thoughts in your mind. In business, overheads are vanity and profits are sanity.

Gary Player

FOLLOW THROUGH

1

To finish first, you must first finish.

—Rick Mears

1988 SENIOR BRITISH OPEN:
TURNBERRY, SCOTLAND

Nineteen eighty-eight was a very special year of senior Majors for me, and it began in spectacular fashion. I had delivered a solid performance in the British Open on the regular tour the week before this at Royal Lytham & St Annes, and I took this confidence with me to the Ailsa Course at Turnberry.

I have always had a passion for links golf. What few people realize is that I love the little stone walls that you find on many links courses. I have carried this through in many of my golf

Playing it as it lies

course designs and have worked in stone walls where I can. On my farm in the Karoo, I have a stone wall that was built by Boer soldiers during the Anglo–Boer War, and whenever I pass it I add a stone of my own.

Links golf demands such a variety of shots, and you have to think very carefully and cleverly from tee to green. As a pure links test, the Ailsa Course at Turnberry encompasses all of the elements that make for great links golf and demands all of the best qualities from its champions.

My love for links golf certainly shone through when I signed for a five-under-par 65 in the first round, which tied the lowest first eighteen-hole score in the history of this championship. I held on to my lead over the next few rounds.

The final round was typically windy, but I made two good birdies on the 12th and 16th holes to beat off a charging Billy Casper and claim a wire-to-wire victory by one stroke.

Another element of links golf that I have always enjoyed is that air of unpredictability. After all, links golf is so much like life itself. You can hit a good shot and get a bad bounce or hit a bad shot and see it kick favorably onto the fairway. There is just something about it.

I've often thought about what makes one golfer different from another. Why is it that I, small as I was and traveling all around the world, could achieve what other golfers, who were perhaps more talented than me, could not? And you can put most of it down to fitness and my work ethic and mental strength. But somewhere there is this thing in golf called "the Intangible." I cannot think of Turnberry anymore without thinking of Tom Watson's magnificent performance in almost winning the Open Championship there in 2009.

I sat riveted to the television, watching that great championship unfold. At the age of fifty-nine, Tom was on the verge of becoming the oldest winner of a Major on the regular tour in the history of golf. He fell short, as we know. But not before a tremendously inspiring performance that had him in the running right up until the closing holes.

What is it that can allow a man of that age to so dominate a host of men younger than him on that stage? What is it in his mind that makes him, at fifty-nine, still so different to the younger players who just had no answer for him that week? That's the Intangible. I believe we may never have the full answer for this beautiful mystery of the game.

THE CHOKE CHALLENGE

Confidence is a key asset in career success, but it means nothing if you don't follow through on that confidence. It is one thing to start well in something, and it is quite another to finish well. My opening 65 was indeed a great start to this Major, and it took its place in the record books. But it would have meant nothing if I went on to lose. Who remembers those players who started well in Majors but didn't go on to win them, even if those starts were records?

A good start means nothing if you don't build on it. Even though I started so well at Turnberry, so much can still take place over four rounds of a Major, and it was still a close finish between Billy Casper and me.

Once you've made that good start, you have to keep going at it, keep gaining the advantage, and never let up until the job is well and truly done.

In business, starting well is simply an indication of intent. Finishing well is an indication of true success.

MAJOR MENTALITY

In golf, the swing is nothing without a good follow-through. The start of your swing is all about intent. It signifies everything you hope to achieve with this particular shot. But the follow-through represents the result.

The same applies to business. You are judged on what you have done, not what you are about to do or set out to do. Finish what you started.

PLAY YOUR OWN GAME

For he that wavereth is like a wave of the sea driven
by the wind and tossed.

—James 1:6

1988 SENIOR PGA CHAMPIONSHIP:
PGA NATIONAL GOLF CLUB, FLORIDA

My fourth senior Major victory reminded me so
much of my earlier successes in Major championships. There were times when one great shot
defined a major triumph for me, and this was another one of
those.

Bob Charles set the early pace and surged five strokes ahead
with an opening round 64. But by the end of the third round, he
had been caught. Chi Chi Rodriguez and Al Geiberger shared
the fifty-four-hole lead, and I was only one stroke behind.

Then, in the final round, I hit an amazing four iron to within inches of the hole on the eighth. The tournament turned in my favor right there, and I went on to win by three shots.

Course management has always been a key element in my success, and the reason for my success in this area of the game is that I never allowed myself to be affected by what others thought or how they believed I should be approaching the game.

Believe me, there were times during my career when staying true to myself was incredibly difficult. During my playing career on the regular tour, I had death threats because I was a South African and therefore perceived to be a supporter of apartheid.

You want to talk about pressure? Well, the most pressure I have ever experienced on a golf course was probably at the 1969 PGA Championship in Dayton, Ohio.

While I played, people were throwing ice in my eyes, telephone books at my back during my backswing, and balls through my legs on the green. They were charging me on the greens when I was about to putt and screaming as I took the putter back. I missed a one footer because of it. I had policemen escorting me around the golf course, walking with me even when I had to go to the bathroom, and sitting with me when I had lunch at the clubhouse. And all those demonstrations cost me the tournament. I lost to Raymond Floyd by one shot because of it.

I played in other tournaments where a police van traveled on the fairway behind me, and they were throwing demonstrators in the back of the van while I was trying to play. I was accused of inventing apartheid. Here I was doing everything in my power to sponsor young black golfers in South Africa and paying for some of them to go play overseas. I was publically calling for the release of Nelson Mandela. But it wasn't recognized.

I did my best to support our nonwhite golfers, such as the talented Indian golfer Sewsunker "Papwa" Sewgolum. Yet when he became the first nonwhite to win a South African golf title in the 1963 Natal Open at Durban Country Club and then had to accept his trophy in the pouring rain because the law did not allow him entry to the clubhouse, it was said that I sat in the clubhouse at the time and did nothing. But I wasn't even there. I never played in that tournament. I was in the United States, and the newspapers verified this.

I was caught between a rock and a hard place. To some, I was not doing enough to break down apartheid, while others felt I was far too liberal in my dealings with black golfers. In those years I walked a fine line of incurring the wrath of the South African government as I persevered at bringing integrated sport into South Africa.

I remember clearly my most daring gamble of all—trying to get Lee Elder to play in South Africa. Elder made a name for himself as the first black professional to play in the Masters. He won four times on the PGA Tour and was a member of the winning Ryder Cup team in 1979.

I felt that to get Elder to play in South Africa would make a strong political statement both overseas and at home. So I arranged a meeting with the South African prime minister, John Vorster, and said, "I want to start international integrated sport in this country. I would like to bring Lee Elder over to this country." He looked at me from under those bushy eyebrows of his, and I thought he was going to throw me out of his office. He'd just stopped a Japanese jockey from riding in South Africa and Basil D'Oliveira from representing South Africa in cricket. How sad. But he said to me, "Go ahead." I got the shock of my life. Elder became the first black PGA Tour member to compete against whites in South Africa, and he participated in a number of exhibition matches with myself around the country.

I was known as a traitor by the ultraright in my own country. There were also many local activists who had their own agendas and who still found a way to criticize me. But you can't pay attention to that. You will always have your critics, and you need to sift the positive criticism from the negative. Make no mistake, unfair criticism has been very hard for me to deal with. It hurts when people who don't even know you say that you did things you know you didn't do. But it's all part of developing a greater temperament and a great character and a strong mind.

You need to have the strength to play your own game, no matter what. And I have always tried to treat jealousy and hatred with love. I remember playing tournaments in the sixties, and the American Black Panther movement was very active in fighting for equal rights for African Americans in the United States. Of course, they were also quite vociferous in their criticism of me as a white South African, and they demonstrated at several tournaments where I played.

So at one of the tournaments, I decided to invite them for tea. We sat down, and I shared with them my views and listened to theirs. We left understanding each other a lot better.

THE CHOKE CHALLENGE

Bob Charles's opening 64 knocked the wind out of most of us. Fear is crippling. The fear of being overshadowed by someone else's achievements is a tremendous obstacle in business. That's when you need to shift the focus away from the other person and back to your own plan. No matter what others are doing, stick to your own plan.

Golf teaches you this like no other sport. Over the four rounds of a Major championship, you cannot play just one man because there are so many factors that go into overall success. You have to deal with the playing conditions, the golf course, and a whole field of competitors. If you teed off the first hole in a Major focused on just beating one man, you would surely lose sight of all the other elements that can prove to be your undoing. Similarly, you cannot control what the rest of the field does. You can control only your own game.

You can't stop somebody from shooting a 64, but you can stop yourself from producing your best performance on the day by being so fixated with somebody else's game. To stick to your plan, you need to have confidence in that plan. Then you need to have the patience to see that plan through. Your chance will come, and when it does you'll be ready to take it. So stick to your plan.

When you are making decisions of great importance, you have to have a calm about you. Watson, Nicklaus, Hogan, and all of the great golfers in the game, when they were playing their best, had a tremendous calm about them. Palmer and Trevino had a different kind of confidence, but that was their calm. Casper had a workmanlike calm, also very different. They would see the shot in their minds, see the end result. The successful businessman does the same. He sees the end result of the path he is on.

In my career, I made a decision, and I went with it. Winston Churchill once said he was never embarrassed at making a mistake because so many people do it. You can worry yourself to death about some mistake you made. Or you can make that adjustment and move on. Ask yourself, "In five years, will anybody care about this?"

MAJOR MENTALITY

Make your plan and stick to it. It's when you move away from your plan that doubt creeps in. And that's when the seeds of choking are sown.

It's so easy to get sidetracked from what you have set out to do. There are so many factors pulling our minds in different directions every single moment of every day. It can be the challenges of juggling a family with your career aspirations. It can be work colleagues feeding you negative thoughts. It can even be your boss, whose own indecision influences your strategy on a particular project.

But trust yourself. After all, that's why you are in the position you are and get paid what you are paid. You are there because somebody believes in your ability to make good decisions. So believe in yourself.

Once you have considered all the necessary information, make your plan and stick to it.

YOU'RE NEVER TOO OLD TO WIN

Gary Player

Fall seven times, stand up eight.

—Japanese proverb

1988 US SENIOR OPEN:
MEDINAH COUNTRY CLUB, ILLINOIS

There is nothing like that feeling of success. It's the most intoxicating feeling in the world, that feeling when everything is going right, and you cannot make a wrong move.

That was how 1988 felt to me. I was reveling in my most successful year as a senior golfer.

Then came that first round at Medinah Country Club.

The course was brutal, as only a US Open course can be. Course #3 has hosted three US Opens and two PGA Championships on the regular tour, and when we played it the rough was typically punishing. That first round in particular, golf proved itself to be the great leveler that it is. I left the golf course with a first round of 74.

Can you imagine? In my best year, I shot my worst round. Golf is the one game where you can go from one day of doing everything right to another of not knowing why everything is going wrong. That 74 was like a mental slap in the face. I was completely shaken by it, and what followed were rounds of 70, 71, and 73—hardly great scoring.

Billy Casper and Walt Zembriski made the early move in this Major with first-round scores of three-under-par 69. Despite my disastrous start, I still managed to hang in there.

In the second round, Casper signed for a 70 to surge ahead by four strokes. Still I just kept hanging in there.

After three rounds, my determination paid off as Casper and I shared the lead at one under par. This was just one of those Majors in which I had to grind out a score every single round.

In the final round, Bob Charles took control, and he was three shots clear of me with four holes to play. But he bogeyed the next three holes; I kept on grinding away and making pars. There are times in Majors where a par feels like a birdie, and this was definitely one of those times.

Bob and I were tied for the lead playing the 18th. We both parred the hole to force a play-off. Then, in that play-off, I somehow managed to find the inspiration for a 68, while Bob signed for a 70.

When I think back on this one, I don't know where I found that 68 on that course. It was a punishing week. But I just kept at it. There are a lot of definitions for the word "determination," but in my mind it always meant just never giving up.

This was one of those Majors that I won because I just refused to go away. And most significant, I had won three of the senior Majors in one year. To this day I am still astounded at the fact that I was mentally strong and fit enough to be able to achieve this. I am particularly proud of this because as a golfer you have a far shorter time frame in which to win senior Majors than regular Majors, and to win three in one year was an achievement I appreciated.

I had also become the second man after Miller Barber to win successive US Senior Opens. I hit sixteen greens in regulation at Medinah. That's not too bad.

THE CHOKE CHALLENGE

At the peak of our powers, it's incredibly difficult to accept the sucker punch that is one bad performance, especially when we are working harder than ever to achieve our goals. Being able to accept sudden setbacks and not let them derail you is a tremendous challenge.

That opening round 74 came out of nowhere and caught me completely by surprise. But I accepted it as such. It was a new playing field, and I adjusted very quickly to it. I went on to successfully defend my US Senior Open title. Yes, it wasn't in the same record-breaking fashion as the previous year. But in golf, as in business, sometimes you need to just accept the playing field for what it is and do the best with what you have. And that's when you have to grind out your success.

People often say to me, "Imagine if you were six feet tall, how much more you could've achieved." But that wouldn't have been the case. The fact that I was small made me grind. It taught me never to give up. It welded a work ethic.

You win only by a little bit anyway. But all that hard work and preparation and the sheer scope and volume of effort you have to put into something are what enable you to win by one shot. And that's all you need to win by.

MAJOR MENTALITY

As golfers, we all know that the game will present us with unexpected surprises, such as a hole in one or a good bounce, as well as bad breaks, such as a sudden gust of wind or a lost ball. We have no choice but to accept the good with the bad and move on to the next shot. You need to readjust and reset your mind for a particular pressure situation.

There will be occasions when you win by a handful of shots and others where you have to grind your way to the smallest margin of victory. Business is all about grinding through the difficult stretches and, to use golf speak, keeping your score ticking over. And it's about never losing focus. It may not feel comfortable, and you may feel completely out of sorts, but as long as you are still in the game and within reach of your goal, then you are on the right track. Sometimes you need to stop being too hard on yourself to be perfect and realize that there will be times when you'll have to do the best with what you have and just keep pushing forward. As strange as it may seem, I believe pressure and stress are good for you. God's plan for every single person that ever lived is to experience them.

THE POWER OF MEMORY

Every man's memory is his private literature.

—**Aldous Huxley**

1990 SENIOR BRITISH OPEN:
TURNBERRY, SCOTLAND

I was back at the scene of my 1988 Senior British Open victory, but the Ailsa Course at Turnberry was in a very different mood this time. The wind was blowing so hard that on the 17th hole of the final round, I hit a driver, three wood, three wood. In the practice round, I hit driver and four wood.

The conditions were incredibly tough, and I left myself with an equally tough challenge. When the final round dawned, it was a wet and miserable day. I was five strokes off the lead. But I battled my way to a five-over-par 75—including shooting five

over for the last six holes—on the last day and managed to beat Deane Beman and Brian Waites by a single stroke.

It has gone down in history as the biggest come-from-behind victory in Senior British Open history.

That whole week I kept reminding myself that while the conditions were vastly different, this was the same golf course I had won on before. And I could do so again.

Always draw on your past experience. What may be routine to you is perhaps foreign to another man. What you are used to going through, another man may see as an insurmountable challenge. Experience allows you to be attuned to something mentally. It lays the bricks and the foundation of your mind.

I have never been blessed with the great business acumen of others. But through my experiences, I can bring values such as common sense and patience to any boardroom. Golf has taught me these qualities. It's taught me to know when to be aggressive and when to be conservative. It's taught me how to know when to play the right shot at the right time and not to be in a hurry to make a decision. These are all qualities that have become a habit of my life in business. I didn't learn them in any university or through any great degree. I was taught them on the golf course. So never be afraid to take your experiences in other spheres of your life and apply them in your career.

Remember, you don't have to go and take a course in time management to understand the pressures any parent faces in juggling work and children.

THE CHOKE CHALLENGE

Business conditions change, but remembering your past successes and drawing on them in difficult times are critical.

I always say, you don't take a Rolls-Royce and try to change it. For example, Ernie Els had a Rolls-Royce of a swing. He and Sam Snead had the two most beautiful, natural swings I've ever seen. The worst thing Ernie Els ever did was to go for swing lessons. He was so good, he didn't need any lessons. He could've taught the teachers. If Els never had a lesson in his life, he would've won at least six Majors by now. But he went to several instructors, and they all told him something different. So subconsciously you get confused and start thinking too much about things that you did automatically anyway.

MAJOR MENTALITY

When you get confused, you get negative. In times like these, you need to remember your past successes. Then, just get out of your own way and let it happen again.

I always found it a boost for my confidence to return to a golf course where I had won before. All those good memories come flooding back, and they can be great for carrying you through difficult stretches.

When you feel your confidence wavering, and those negative thoughts start creeping in, just call on a few of your past successes.

The message is simple: If you did it before, you can certainly do it again.

Gary Player

LOVE THE BATTLE ¹

Let not your mind run on what you lack
as much as on what you have already.
Of the things you have, select the best;
and then reflect how eagerly they
would have been sought if you did not have them.

—Marcus Aurelius

1990 SENIOR PGA CHAMPIONSHIP:
PGA NATIONAL GOLF CLUB, FLORIDA

The 1990 Senior PGA Championship, like so many early in my career, summed up my life. I was a lot older and playing against one of the strongest fields assembled for the oldest senior tournament in the game. And I responded positively.

In the third round I went out with a front nine of 29 on my way to a 65. I went on to win with a total of seven-under-par 281, beating Chi Chi Rodriguez by two strokes and Jack Nicklaus and Lee Trevino by four.

I've often said that I feel it was harder to win a Major in my era than it is now. This may seem like a bold statement to make, but there are several reasons for this.

The equipment is better today, and the golf ball flies farther. Before a round we used to take our golf balls and pass them through a ring. If they went through, they were put in our bag. If they didn't fit through the ring, then it meant they were out of shape, and they went into the practice bag because they weren't fit to be used in tournament play.

Then you have to look at the quality of the golf courses and their conditioning. We didn't have the mowers they use today, which present these immaculate fairways and greens for the players.

A few years ago I remember playing in the Masters and hearing of a major bust-up between Vijay Singh and Phil Mickelson and accusations of spike marks on the greens. They almost came to blows in the locker room about it. I played in that Masters, and I remember thinking, "What spike marks? If these are spike marks, then you'd hate to have seen what we played on."

And then you go back even further to the time of Bobby Jones. I've stood on golf courses where Jones hit some of the finest shots in his career, and I cannot fathom how he managed to do it while playing with such inferior equipment.

But perhaps the most significant factor of all is the depth of potential Major winners we had in each field. If I choked in any

Major, you can bet there would have been at least nine players ready to take advantage. We had any number of great champions in our time, and the competition was fierce.

In my opinion, it was harder for Jack Nicklaus to win those eighteen Majors than it's been for Tiger Woods to win his fourteen. Much harder. No comparison. If Nicklaus made a mistake, he was going to get beat. And those around him went on to win a lot of Majors, not just one, two, or three. And think about this: Jack Nicklaus finished second in nineteen Majors.

THE CHOKE CHALLENGE

If you look at the top fifty names on world golf's money list today, there is not a huge difference in their individual play. The difference is in their mental approaches and how consistently they can remain mentally stronger than the opposition.

It was often said of me that I did the most with the little I was given. You take what you are given, and you do the best with it. It's as simple as that. What people don't realize is what I had inside, which one must remember is more important than a great swing. I had great course management and never was a "feel sorry for yourself" competitor.

Some of golf's greatest players never completed the career grand slam (Watson, Palmer, Snead, Floyd, and Trevino), and some reached the great heights only to lose their game completely (Watson, who got his championship game back, Ian Baker-Finch, and David Duval). Why did this happen to them, but not to Jack, Tiger, or me?

A key element in not choking is understanding the role of competition and adversaries in your life and career.

Often, people who choke don't enjoy the competition. They see their adversaries as an obstacle to the enjoyment of their careers, rather than viewing them as an inspiration. I, however, looked at all the great champions that I played with and against, and I viewed them as the reasons for me to keep improving. As long as there was somebody ready to take my place, I had to make sure I was better. And my adversaries also became my great friends.

To this day Jack Nicklaus and I are great friends. When I showed him the golf course I built on my farm in the Karoo in South Africa, I also showed him a particular hole that I had named "Cactus Jack" in honor of him. We had a plaque made and mounted it on one of the rocks near the tee, and Jack was there to officially open the hole as part of a small ceremony between our families.

The funny thing is that when I have breakfast on the farm, sitting under this huge oak tree in my garden and with my two favorite dogs lying beside me, the sun shines on that plaque, and the glare can almost blind you.

So I said to Jack, "Man, if it wasn't bad enough that I had to play against you all of those years, now you're still in my face and blinding me when I have breakfast on my farm." We had a good laugh about that.

The quality of your adversaries says a lot about you as a competitor.

MAJOR MENTALITY

People often ask me if I'd rather have played in this era, what with all the money in the game, and I can honestly say no. The competition in our time was tough, no doubt about it. We also didn't have a lot of the luxuries today's professionals enjoy. But it made you even tougher as a competitor. And life is tough. The "ifs" don't count.

I cannot thank my fellow competitors enough for teaching me this. Ben Hogan won nine Majors. He played during a time when traveling by air was an ordeal, as jets were not yet in use; he survived a horrific car accident, and the doctors swore he would never play again; and he did a stint in the Army during the prime of his career. His determination and will were fantastic and set an example for me to aspire to equal.

Life is a challenge, and you need to embrace this, not shy away from it. It's these challenges that reveal to us the most about ourselves and that make our successes that much more rewarding.

WITH GREAT SUCCESS COMES GREAT RESPONSIBILITY

Gary Player

Against criticism a man can neither protest nor defend himself;
he must act in spite of it, and then it will gradually yield to him.

—Johann Wolfgang von Goethe

1997 SENIOR BRITISH OPEN:
ROYAL PORTRUSH, NORTHERN IRELAND

I was sixty-two years old in 1997, an age at which most people consider their competitive lives to be over. Yet here I was, on the brink of making history. I had happiness and security in my business and family life, and I was perfectly positioned for this moment.

The weather was typically cold and windy, but I managed to open with a 68, which put me two shots behind my countryman John Bland at the top of the leaderboard. After the second

Sinking the putt to win the 1997 Senior British Open.

round Australian Noel Ratcliffe held the halfway lead following a spectacular 65, but he faded by shooting a 75 in the third round.

The tournament eventually became a head-to-head battle between John and me. We finished tied for the lead at ten under par, taking us into a sudden-death play-off.

It is never easy going up against a good friend in such a situation. But I didn't let such thoughts detract me from a career-defining achievement. On the first play-off hole, the par-five 17th, I made birdie by sinking a fifteen-foot putt that broke six inches left to right. Then I birdied the 18th on the second play-off hole, and it was done. I had equaled my nine Major victories on the regular tour. I had become the only winner of the career Grand Slam on the regular tour and the senior tour.

It was a tremendous accomplishment that I am truly very proud of, but I have always believed that humility is a great asset in life. I'll never forget Nelson Mandela, the first president of a democratic South Africa, arriving one year by helicopter at my Gary Player Invitational tournament in South Africa, which raises funds for underprivileged children. I met him at the helicopter in a golf cart, and as the doors opened, he said to me, "Gary, do you still remember me?" There he was, one of the most famous men in the world, but he was filled with such humility. There was no revenge, no hatred in his heart. In all the time I spent with him, love was what he exuded.

I've traveled around the world and seen people living in desperate circumstances. And every time, it makes me realize that if you've got a roof over your head and clothes and food, then you've won the lottery compared to what some people have.

I think it's imperative for people who have something to share with people who have little. We can all make an effort at giving something or anything that can create love and hope for people. Everybody needs to have hope. So think of giving back. If you can improve one person's life, you have made a phenomenal difference in the world. Every time I saw President Mandela, I cried. I have so much respect and love for him. I suppose subconsciously I knew what he went through.

THE CHOKE CHALLENGE

I had achieved everything there was for me to achieve in the game. I had distinguished myself in golf, in life, and in my business.

When I was younger, if you had asked me how I would like to be remembered, I would have told you as a great golfer. But now, if I am to be remembered at all, I would like it to be as a person who made a difference in this world beyond just the playing of golf.

It keeps haunting me of how I struggled as a young child. I can't think of anything worse than a child who is suffering. I always said that if I ever became successful, I was going to help some children have some sweetness in their lives.

The Gary Player Invitational series of tournaments around the world has been an amazing vehicle for us to raise funds for charities involved in fighting poverty and obesity among children and assisting with their education. Since 1983, the international series has raised over $30 million for such initiatives. We play tournaments in the United Kingdom, the United States, China, and South Africa, and we receive amazing support from golfers, businesspeople, and celebrities.

And it makes a huge difference in the lives of the people we are helping. A few years ago, I visited a school for settlement-area children in Cape Town, South Africa, and it left an indelible imprint on my mind.

I rank that day as one of the top five days of my life. When we visited this school, the children received me so warmly. They sang a song for me, and many of them knew all about my career, which shocked me. I was so choked up by the fact that these kids had never slept between two white sheets, never sat on a proper toilet or in a proper bath, never gone to school in a car. But they still had this amazing optimism.

I felt so encouraged that our country could produce these children under such difficult circumstances. When I left, the kids hugged me and wouldn't let go. I got in the car and cried like a baby. To be able to raise money for people who need it—that's very special. On my farm in South Africa, I built a small church and school, and we host an annual sports day for the local children.

And then you have moments when you realize the difference you have made in someone's life. In 2007, I was walking in the Cape Town city center, and I heard somebody call my name. I looked behind me, and there was nobody. Then I heard it again. After a while I looked up, and a black man was leaning out of an office window. He shouted down at me, "Thank you, Gary. I've got this great job because of the education you gave me."

You never forget moments like that, just as you never forget struggling.

MAJOR MENTALITY

True success is judged by your relationship with your fellow human beings. This life is about making a difference. It's not about personal enrichment or glory. Someone once said that we are blessed so that we can be a blessing to others.

In business, I was driven to succeed so that I could pass this success on to those I wanted to help. To simply garner success for yourself can become a very unrewarding experience. Your success needs to positively affect others for it to have wide-ranging benefits for society as a whole. And this is within reach of one person in a career, a small business, or the biggest multinational corporations.

THE NINETEENTH MAJOR: FITNESS AND NUTRITION

O n my farm in the Little Karoo of South Africa, my day begins at dawn when I step into the gym I have there and start my workout. I put on my favorite country music and go about my exercise program.

Some would say I have an obsession with physical fitness. I have even been dubbed "Mr. Fitness," and early in my life and career, I was branded crazy for the way in which I advocated physical fitness in golf. Having made it a priority in my life for so long, I wouldn't say I'm obsessed with it. It just seems the most normal thing for me to do. To be honest, I don't know if I could start a day any other way.

Wherever I travel in the world, I preach the benefits of a healthy lifestyle and physical fitness routine. I do so because I am living proof of these benefits. And I know that at the highest level of competition, being fit and healthy leads to a stronger mind and less chance of choking. By being fit you are an asset to your

2009 Legends of Golf with Bob Charles

country, family, business, and to yourself. Fitness breeds productivity. The more physically fit a person is, the more mentally fit he or she will also be.

You see, it's all interlinked. How you handle a pressure situation is largely based on what you feed your mind. And the strength of your mind can also be improved by what you feed your body.

There were so many times coming down the stretch in a Major where just knowing I was in better physical shape than my opponent gave me the mental strength and confidence I needed to beat him. Exercise and nutrition have been key ingredients in my success. I've often said that exercise is the king and nutrition the queen.

If you look at the average Western diet, we treat our bodies criminally. A DVD called *Eating* has had a profound effect on me, particularly one scene of a cow that included the words, "You killed me, but I will kill you from the grave with the cholesterol and fat I'm pumping into your body."

Every year I learn to eat better, and I am eating better now than ever before in my life. On my farm I have a huge vegetable garden, and slowly but surely I am attempting to become a hundred percent vegetarian. Doctors at the Mayo and Cleveland clinics have stated that if people were to stay away from animal

Holing out at the 2009 Masters Par 3 tournament.

fats and embrace vegetarianism, cancer would become a disease of the past. I believe them.

When I travel and order lunch, waiters look at me as if I am mad. I tell them I want a handful of rice, sliced tomatoes, sliced avocado, sliced cucumber, one grated carrot, one slice of rough whole wheat bread, and a cup of herbal tea with honey.

All it takes is a little planning, and you can eat very healthily no matter where you find yourself in the world. With all the traveling I do, I often have my own little "emergency" pack of food with me, including dried fruit and nuts, whole grain crackers, and bottled water. This is always a healthy way to fill a gap when you can't find a decent meal. But there are so many healthier food options nowadays than were available early in my career. And wherever I find myself in the world, my menu selection is based on some sound principles, namely, always choosing the low-fat option and ensuring I get plenty of vegetables. And for breakfast I always opt for the fresh fruit, green juice, oatmeal, and whole wheat toast.

The responsibility of what you eat is entirely in your own hands, and it is possible to enjoy a wonderful life of good food, if you select the healthy options.

Your body is the most amazing instrument you will ever own or use, and I discovered this early in my life. My older brother Ian and I were always competing. There was one occasion where he beat me badly in a race, and he literally kicked my butt because I had lost by so much to him. During the race I was so tired that I sat down and told Ian "I can't." He wrote "can't" in the dirt with a stick, crossed out the "t," and kicked me in the butt. I got up and finished the race.

There and then I became determined to get as strong and fit as I possibly could. Being smaller than most of my competitors, I knew that being in better shape gave me an edge over them. I resolved that in a pressure situation, while so many other variables may come into it and may affect the outcome, my body was the one thing that was not going to let me down. I was never going to allow myself to be in a situation where I felt tired or fatigued. I get so upset when I hear TV commentators say how tired a golfer is. Having said this, I have always believed that tiredness is largely a condition of the mind. I believe that if you exercise, eat correctly, and rest properly, you should never be tired. I have traveled more

than any athlete in the history of the world, and I have never suffered from such fatigue that I feel like I cannot compete.

When I hear golfers saying they are tired, I use the following example to prove that it's largely in their minds that they are tired. Say you told me you were physically exhausted. Then say I offered you a million dollars to fly to another country and play in a tournament there. Most people immediately would say, "Sure, I'll do it." So a moment ago they were physically exhausted. But now suddenly they're feeling fit and strong again. This is what makes me believe that, under normal conditions, tiredness is merely a condition of the mind.

My friends and business associates have always joked about my ability to overcome jet lag, and physical exercise is the answer to my secret. I know that the gym is the key to my quality of life and my ability to continue playing the game that is so enjoyable for me and traveling and meeting as many people as I do. I speak of my exercise "routine," but I have always been very careful not to turn it into too much of a routine.

To really push your body physically and get the best out of it, you need to keep varying your exercise program. But there are certain fundamentals that you will need to master and include in your daily exercise program. I've always said that every strong building has a strong foundation. For the golfer, this strong foundation is the legs. Strong upper thighs, hamstrings, and glutes (your buttocks muscles) are critical for power and stability in the golf swing.

The first time I saw Jack Nicklaus hit a ball, I could not believe how powerful his legs were. For a start, his thighs were at least the size of my waist. The power Jack generated with those legs was scary.

The torso is also critical to power, stability, and posture in the golf swing. This is often referred to as core training. Every workout I do incorporates a great deal of training for my abdominals. Not only are the abdominals critical for generating swing speed, they are also the protector of the lower back. When you combine great leg strength with a strong torso, you are able to swing powerfully while holding the correct posture throughout the entire swing.

Now, while it's true that the big muscles—the legs and torso—are the greatest source of power in the swing, the hands, arms, and shoulders are also important for power and, perhaps more important, for feel. I have always believed that strong hands, forearms, and triceps are critical to the swing.

Arnold Palmer had the strongest hands and forearms that you could imagine. I have told the story many times of when Arnold, in his prime, visited South Africa with me. We went on a tour of the gold mines. There was a brick of gold that the gentleman conducting the tour boldly proclaimed could be taken home by anyone who could pick it up with one hand and carry it out. Well, Arnold walked right over, grabbed it in his big paw, and began to walk right out of the room. I'll never forget the look on that tour guide's face. It was no coincidence that Arnold was such a great driver of the golf ball and could slash it out even from the thickest of roughs.

Flexibility has always been a key focus area in my fitness. I work very hard at keeping my hamstrings loose. When your hamstrings are tight, your entire torso, especially the lower back, suffers.

People often complain about not having proper access to a gym or exercise equipment and so on. I have traveled around the world and worked out in some great gyms and some pretty

awful ones, but I will tell you that as long as you have a set of dumbbells and an exercise mat, there is a way to push your body through a very effective workout. And even if you don't have access to this equipment, you can always improvise if the desire is there. I remember moving beds around in my hotel room and using them to do my exercises.

If you want to be fully armed against the possibility of choking in a pressure situation, then exercise and eating right has to become a way of life. It is difficult at first, but you will find that once you get into a routine, your body will crave the workout. Stick with it, and you will begin to enjoy life like never before. And remember, there is no quick-fix solution. Your body is not some sort of fast-food drive-through where you can just order what you want and move on. The only way is through hard work and dedication.

People who think they can perform better or choke less by using performance-enhancing drugs are deluded. Yet steroid use is prevalent in our society. And not just among professional athletes. Our schools are riddled with young children who have sold out to society's concept of fulfilling a dream quickly.

My career is a perfect example of how far plain old hard work can get you. And my record in the senior Majors is an example for all to realize the importance of fitness and the lasting power thereof. After the age of fifty, I was able to win nine senior Majors, three of them in the same year in 1988. That shows how fit you have got to be, particularly because these Majors are not played on the same continent.

And I was also the oldest player to make the cut at the 1995 Open Championship at the age of fifty-nine and the oldest at the 1998 Masters at the age of sixty-two, and I competed in fifty-two Masters tournaments.

My ambition is to take this message to two or three hundred million young people—eat properly, rest well, and exercise. Get an education, use good manners, and honor your mother and father.

Feed the mind. Feed the body. Don't choke.

Gary Player's Super Foods to Prevent Choking

Spinach
Wheat grass
Brussels sprouts
Cabbage
Garlic
Onions
Water with a pH of 6 or more
Brown bread
Honey
Fruit
Vegetables
Red peppers for vitamin C
Avoid
High fat and sugar foods

EPILOGUE

A cool wind blows over him as he sits down under a large oak tree on his farm, overlooking the great expanse of the Karoo beyond.

The air is filled with the powerful voice of Luciano Pavarotti and his rendition of "Nessun Dorma" (none shall sleep).

He closes his eyes.

"I have not failed to get the most of out every day of my life," he says. "You talk about a legacy to the game. Forget about being a great golfer. I'd like to be remembered as a man who loved people, who loved life, and who tried to contribute to society."

And it's still the little things that stand out in a career of mythical proportion. Little things like a cricket bat from school.

"At school, in Grade 11, I was voted the Best All-Round Sportsman in the entire school. I played first team rugby and first team cricket, I was awarded half colors for athletics and

swimming, and I did boxing and horseback riding. I won a cricket bat as my award. It's still one of the great achievements of my life."

Later that day, he walks the nine-hole golf course that he is building on his farm. It's his vision of the world's first golf course that is eighty percent water free. For now, it's the vision of one man and the seven farm laborers who have worked with him to build this golf course.

It's a new vision. He is seventy-four years old. But there is a new vision.

"I've always got a reason."

None shall sleep.

But when he does, it is to a silent prayer:

I asked for strength,

And God gave me difficulties to make me strong.

I prayed for wisdom,

And God gave me problems to solve.

I asked for prosperity,

And God gave me brains and strength to work.

I prayed for courage,

And God gave me dangers to overcome.

I asked for love,

And God gave me opportunities.

I asked for humility,

And God gave me experiences not to be proud of.

I asked God to grant me patience,

And God said, "No."

He said that patience is a product of tribulation.

It is not granted. It is earned.

I asked God to spare me pain,

2009 Masters 18th hole. The last hole at the Masters ever played. >>

And God said, "No."

He said, "Suffering draws you apart from worldly cares
And brings you closer to me."

I received nothing I wanted.

I received everything I needed.

My prayer has been answered.

ACKNOWLEDGMENTS

Throughout the vast majority of my career, I was considered to be "a bit of a nutter" because of my dedication to the mental aspect of the game and especially diet, health, and fitness. But in the end it was this dedication that allowed me to win eighteen Major championships and the career Grand Slam on the European, PGA, European Senior, and Champions tours.

The foundation I was given I owe to the people who provided me with the love, support, motivation, and knowledge to succeed when everyone in the golf world told me that I never could or would.

My father taught me two important things that have always stayed with me—be dedicated and always believe that you can be the best. He worked miles underground in the gold mines in horrid conditions, but every day he got up and went to work

to support his family. When I was just starting to play golf, he was the one who pushed me to practice and to devote myself to winning.

My mother taught me to love unconditionally—something everyone should learn.

My brother Ian, a great conservationist and one of my best friends, taught me that I *can* when I think I *can't*.

My sister Wilma gave me the gift that probably had the most profound effect on how I look at life—Norman Vincent Peale's book *The Power of Positive Thinking*. I can say without a doubt that it changed my life.

Vivienne, my beloved wife, helped me be a better man and raised our family almost single-handedly. I was traveling so much it was nearly impossible for me to be an everyday father, and Vivienne kept our family together and raised six wonderful children and twenty-one grandchildren. Can you imagine a wife traveling with six children tourist class, no jets, forty hours to America or Australia? What a woman.

My in-laws taught me what it means to give total support to those who become part of a family. Early in my career, when none of us knew for sure that I would make it as a professional golfer, their unwavering belief in my abilities and support to our family helped me get through those days when doubt started to creep into my mind.

I owe thanks to my son Marc and the team at Black Knight International, who worked so hard to get this book published.

I also want to pay special thanks to Dr. Bob Rotella, who was kind enough to write the foreword to this book. His insight into the mind and what it takes to succeed is inspirational.

And last, but certainly not least, I want to thank Michael Vlismas for helping me to write this book. The hours we spent together reliving the stories contained in this book brought back such powerful and wonderful memories. Thank you. Memories are the cushions of life.

—**Gary Player**

Gary Player

MY MAJOR CHAMPIONSHIPS

1

1959 BRITISH OPEN: MUIRFIELD, SCOTLAND

284 Gary Player (South Africa) 75-71-70-68

286 Fred Bullock (Great Britain) 68-70-74-74, Flory Van Donck (Belgium) 70-70-73-73

1961 MASTERS: AUGUSTA NATIONAL GOLF CLUB, GEORGIA

280 Gary Player (South Africa) 69-68-69-74

281 Arnold Palmer (United States) 68-69-73-71, Charles Coe (United States, amateur) 72-71-69-69

1962 PGA CHAMPIONSHIP: ARONIMINK GOLF CLUB, PENNSYLVANIA

278 Gary Player (South Africa) 72-67-69-70

279 Bob Goalby (United States) 69-72-71-67

1965 US OPEN: BELLERIVE COUNTRY CLUB, MISSOURI

*282 *Gary Player (South Africa) 70-70-71-71, Kel Nagle
(Australia) 68-73-72-69*

(* Player won in the eighteen-hole play-off with a score of 71 to Nagle's 74.)

1968 BRITISH OPEN: CARNOUSTIE, SCOTLAND

289 Gary Player (South Africa) 74-71-71-73

*291 Jack Nicklaus (United States) 76-69-73-73, Bob Charles (New
Zealand) 72-72-71-76*

**1972 PGA CHAMPIONSHIP: OAKLAND HILLS
COUNTRY CLUB, MICHIGAN**

281 Gary Player (South Africa) 71-71-67-72

*283 Tommy Aaron (United States) 71-71-70-71, Jim Jamieson
(United States) 69-72-72-70*

**1974 MASTERS: AUGUSTA NATIONAL GOLF CLUB,
GEORGIA**

278 Gary Player (South Africa) 71-71-66-70

*280 Dave Stockton (United States) 71-66-70-73, Tom Weiskopf
(United States) 71-69-70-70*

**1974 BRITISH OPEN: ROYAL LYTHAM & ST
ANNES, ENGLAND**

282 Gary Player (South Africa) 69-68-75-70

286 Peter Oosterhuis (Great Britain) 71-71-73-71

**1978 MASTERS: AUGUSTA NATIONAL GOLF CLUB,
GEORGIA**

277 Gary Player (South Africa) 72-72-69-64

*278 Rod Funseth (United States) 73-66-70-69, Hubert Green
(United States) 72-69-65-72, Tom Watson (United States)
73-68-68-69*

**1986 SENIOR PGA CHAMPIONSHIP: PGA
NATIONAL GOLF CLUB, FLORIDA**

281 Gary Player (South Africa)

283 Lee Elder (United States)

1987 SENIOR TPC: SAWGRASS COUNTRY CLUB, FLORIDA

280 Gary Player (South Africa)

281 Bruce Crampton (Australia), Chi Chi Rodriguez (Puerto Rico)

1987 US SENIOR OPEN: BROOKLAWN COUNTRY CLUB, CONNECTICUT

270 Gary Player (South Africa)

276 Doug Sanders (United States)

1988 SENIOR BRITISH OPEN: TURNBERRY, SCOTLAND

272 Gary Player (South Africa)

273 Billy Casper (United States)

1988 SENIOR PGA CHAMPIONSHIP: PGA NATIONAL GOLF CLUB, FLORIDA

284 Gary Player (South Africa)

287 Chi Chi Rodriguez (Puerto Rico)

1988 US SENIOR OPEN: MEDINAH COUNTRY CLUB, ILLINOIS

288 ★Gary Player (South Africa), Bob Charles (New Zealand)

(★ Player won in an eighteen-hole play-off.)

1990 SENIOR BRITISH OPEN: TURNBERRY, SCOTLAND

280 Gary Player (South Africa)

281 Dean Beman (United States), Brian Waites (Great Britain)

1990 SENIOR PGA CHAMPIONSHIP: PGA NATIONAL GOLF CLUB, FLORIDA

281 Gary Player (South Africa)

283 Chi Chi Rodriguez (Puerto Rico)

1997 SENIOR BRITISH OPEN: ROYAL PORTRUSH, NORTHERN IRELAND

278 *Gary Player (South Africa)

278 John Bland (South Africa)

(* Player won on second play-off hole.)

Gary Player

1

BIBLIOGRAPHY

Barrett, Ted. *The Chronicle of Golf.* London: Carlton Books, 1994.

Locke, Bobby. *Bobby Locke on Golf.* London: Country Life Limited, 1953.

Player, Gary. *Grand Slam Golf.* London: Cassell, 1966 and *Success* London: David Charle 1982.

Player, Gary. *Gary Player on Fitness.*

Player, Gary. *The Complete Golfer's Handbook.* London: New Holland, 1999.

Player, Gary. *Player* magazine. August 15, 2004.

Smart, Ted. *The Illustrated Encyclopedia of Golf.* London: Robert Green and HarperCollins, 1994.

Swanepoel, Anton. *Play Your Business Like a Pro.* Vanderbijlpark: Carpe Diem, 2005.